# White Mountains State

### A Four-Year Journey Hiking and Summiting
### New Hampshire's 48 Highest Peaks

*DAVID,*

*THANK YOU FOR ALL YOU'VE*
*DONE FOR NEW BOSTON. AND*
*thank you FOR supporting*
*THE BEACON.*

## Keith Gentili

**White Mountains State**
**A Four-Year Journey Hiking and Summiting**
**New Hampshire's 48 Highest Peaks**

Copyright © Keith Gentili 2022

ISBN: 978-1-7349308-8-7

731 Tasker Hill Rd.
Conway, NH 03818
USA
www.tmcbooks.com

Dedication

For my partners on trail—Eric, Eric, Keith, Jake, and Ron—whose support, trust, and enthusiasm made the journey so much greater than the destination every time out. And for my partners in life—Carrie, Julia, and Sarah—for whom it all matters. Put it on the board.

# NEW HAMPSHIRE 48
## In order of elevation

| | | | |
|---|---|---|---|
| 1. | Washington, 6,288 ft. | 25. | Flume, 4,328 ft. |
| 2. | Adams, 5,799 ft. | 26. | South Hancock, 4,319 ft. |
| 3. | Jefferson, 5,716 ft. | 27. | Pierce, 4,312 ft. |
| 4. | Monroe, 5,372 ft. | 28. | North Kinsman, 4,293 ft. |
| 5. | Madison, 5,366 ft. | 29. | Willey, 4,285 ft. |
| 6. | Lafayette, 5,260 ft. | 30. | Bondcliff, 4,265 ft. |
| 7. | Lincoln, 5,089 ft. | 31. | Zealand, 4,260 ft. |
| 8. | South Twin, 4,902 ft. | 32. | North Tripyramid, 4,180 ft. |
| 9. | Carter Dome, 4,832 ft. | 33. | Cabot, 4,170 ft. |
| 10. | Moosilauke, 4,802 ft. | 34. | East Osceola, 4,156 ft. |
| 11. | North Twin, 4,761 ft. | 35. | Middle Tripyramid, 4,140 ft. |
| 12. | Eisenhower, 4,760 ft. | 36. | Cannon, 4,100 ft. |
| 13. | Carrigain, 4,700 ft. | 37. | Wildcat D, 4,062 ft. |
| 14. | Bond, 4,698 ft. | 38. | Hale, 4,054 ft. |
| 15. | Middle Carter, 4,610 ft. | 39. | Jackson, 4,052 ft. |
| 16. | West Bond, 4,540 ft. | 40. | Tom, 4,051 ft. |
| 17. | Garfield, 4,500 ft. | 41. | Moriah, 4,049 ft. |
| 18. | Liberty, 4,459 ft. | 42. | Passaconaway, 4,043 ft. |
| 19. | South Carter, 4,430 ft. | 43. | Owl's Head, 4,025 ft. |
| 20. | Wildcat, 4,422 ft. | 44. | Galehead, 4,024 ft. |
| 21. | Hancock, 4,420 ft. | 45. | Whiteface, 4,020 ft. |
| 22. | South Kinsman, 4,358 ft. | 46. | Waumbek, 4,006 ft. |
| 23. | Field, 4,340 ft. | 47. | Isolation, 4,003 ft. |
| 24. | Osceola, 4,340 ft. | 48. | Tecumseh, 4,003 ft.* |

*In 2019, a new summit marker was placed atop Mount Tecumseh with an elevation of 3,997 feet. Its status among the NH 48 continues to be a popular topic of debate within the hiking community.

# NEW HAMPSHIRE 48
## 4,000-foot peaks

The memories of a man in his old age
Are the deeds of a man in his prime

Songwriter: Roger Waters of Pink Floyd

# CONTENTS

# INTRODUCTION

On May 18, 2012, I hiked New Hampshire's Franconia Ridge Loop. I was 45 years old, married with two young daughters, a 10-year resident of New Boston, New Hampshire (NH), and a lifelong hiker, but I had never traversed these renowned 8.4 miles. More specifically, I had never experienced the 1.7-mile ridge that runs between the summits of Mount Lafayette and Little Haystack Mountain. It made an impact on me that changed my life.

Six weeks later, on the Fourth of July, I shared the experience of that hike with a friend from town, Brad Bingham. I thought Brad, an accomplished triathlete, might be interested in hearing about the Franconia Ridge Loop, especially the difficulty of the descent down the Falling Waters Trail, which was wet from a recent rain. But while I was stringing hiking anecdotes together, and simultaneously keeping an eye on our kids swimming in a large above-ground pool, Brad interjected with, "My uncle climbed the New Hampshire 48. You should do that."

A few short hours later, I was Googling "New Hampshire 48." And, four years later, on the eve of my 48th birthday—September 26, 2015—accompanied by three of my five hiking partners, I completed the New Hampshire 48 by summiting Mount Carrigain. When I awoke the next morning, a bit hungover from the night's celebration at Schilling Beer Company's Oktoberfest in Littleton, NH, I was 48 years old and a 48er: someone who successfully climbs up and down the 48 White Mountains in New Hampshire higher than 4,000 feet as recognized by the Appalachian Mountain Club (AMC).

What happened between May 18, 2012, and September 26, 2015, proved to be a four-year journey in adventure, higher education, and, most of all, self-discovery. One worth documenting and one that was shared, in part, on social media each step of the way. In fact, all 26 hikes featured in *White Mountains State* were noted via Facebook posts that are also shared here in an effort to present a sense of the moment as it happened.

Each of the journey's four years was unique and the lessons learned mirrored the arc of college life. For example, a freshman-year prerequisite was visiting the bookstore and buying the proper White Mountains-related hiking books and maps. Sophomore year included mastering the campus including all the best parking lots and trailheads as well as the specific routes that would ensure the greatest "bang for the buck." Junior year was about locating the ideal post-hike dining commons based on mood, weather, and time of year. Senior year was bittersweet, as an exit strategy was formed along with graduation plans and plans for after graduation.

It's why this book is broken into four sections—Freshman Year, Sophomore Year, Junior Year, and Senior Year. During each year, significant milestones were reached, such as the introductions of solo hiking, night hiking, winter hiking, and backpacking. These were all natural evolutions in the adventure's curriculum but, like the gear purchased along the way, they were also huge game changers. Plus, a level of expertise was slowly and methodically established, thanks to a genuine commitment to the coursework.

On April 16, 2016, I attended the Appalachian Mountain Club Four Thousand Footer Club annual dinner and graduation ceremony. That night, nearly 900 hikers were recognized across the AMC's six lists including the New Hampshire 48. The diploma is real: it's framed and hangs in my home, symbolizing a unique moment in time when I achieved a significant personal goal.

This book tells the story of 26 hikes and 48 mountains, all 4,000 feet and higher. It also tells the story of the relationships surrounding the journey. Not only the evolving dynamic among hiking partners but also the investment of self, family, and friends. You will hear from all of the people who went along for the ride with me. This includes both my hiking partners and my family.

On trail, I have always said, "Not all miles are created equal." The same is true for life. This adventure was a four-year education, one of mind and body. One I call *White Mountains State*. It was completed successfully thanks to the unique combination of a White Mountains State of Mind and White Mountains State of Play, and it all took place on the campus of White Mountains State University.

—Keith Gentili
May 30, 2022

# ORIENTATION: THE FIRST PEAK

The words popped off the page. Best Alpine Hike. I was immediately attracted. I saw them while flipping through the May 2009 issue of Backpacker magazine and its cover story titled "America's Best Dayhikes." It was on page 76, in the Northeast section. Best Alpine Hike.

The next line identified the location, Franconia Ridge, NH. Now I was biting. And then, *"Get a taste of the Alps in New Hampshire on this high-wire loop. Franconia Ridge's exposed 1.7-mile alpine traverse—over Little Haystack Mountain, Mt. Lincoln, and Mt. Lafayette—feels much higher than its 5,000-foot elevation."*

Boom. I was hooked. I just couldn't stop thinking about tasting the Alps and what that even meant. Although I wasn't sure, I knew I wanted more than just a taste. I wanted to fully consume them. After all, the Franconia Ridge sits less than two hours from my home in New Boston, NH, and I had been looking for something like this for some time.

The fact that the May 2009 issue of *Backpacker* even ended up in my hands is a bit of miracle in itself. My mother, living in Englewood, Florida, did a nice, grandmotherly thing. She bought some magazines through a New Boston elementary school PTA fundraiser to help my daughter Julia score a stuffed caterpillar. While my mom certainly did not purchase *Backpacker*, the program included complimentary issues of other publications. Sort of a buy-one, get-one (BOGO) sampler in hopes folks will like something they see and purchase additional items. As a reminder, in 2009, magazine sales were plummeting as more and more people turned to reading online. Publishers were constantly seeking ways to fuel circulation. This was just one of their strategies.

Well, my mother, being a boat owner living on central Florida's west coast, didn't have much use for *Backpacker* and opted to mail it north in a manila envelope to her youngest son living in southern New Hampshire. However, it took her a few years to get it to me as I didn't receive that envelope until March of 2012. From the moment I read, *"Get a taste of the Alps,"* I knew it was only a matter of time until I did. I hiked the Franconia Ridge Loop on May 18, 2012.

While I didn't know it at the time, that trek became the official start of my New Hampshire 48, hiking all 4,000-foot summits in the Granite State as recognized by the Appalachian Mountain Club (AMC). But it is not where my hiking story begins. By that time, while not avid, I was a regular hiker with a couple of annual peak-bagging trips on my calendar. Of particular note, I had summited Maine's Katahdin (5,269 feet) in 1994 from the east and in 1999 from the west.

That first hike up Katahdin was epic. From Roaring Brook Campground to Chimney Pond, up Cathedral, across Baxter Peak and the Knife Edge, down Helon Taylor Trail, it was a 10-mile loop of sensory overload. It was like being dropped into a postcard with permission to move about freely. And while I embraced everything that day, my hiking partner Steve West got beat down by the final three-mile hike out. The stretch from Pamola Peak back to the car just wore him down and he retired his hiking boots before we reached the Baxter State Park gatehouse at Togue Pond.

Katahdin 1994

In 2000, I hiked Vermont's highest peak, Mount Mansfield (4,393 feet) and, in 2006, I climbed the Northeast's biggest mountain, Mount Washington (6,288 feet), and, unknowingly, New Hampshire 4,000-footer #1, aka The First Peak. The Mount Washington climb was important. It was part of an annual trip that features a group of college friends taking on the outdoors the weekend before Memorial Day. During previous trips, we hiked together in Virginia, West Virginia, New York, Vermont, Maine, and Massachusetts. It made sense we take on the Whites.

That year, 2006, was our 11th annual Outdoor Adventure (OA), and after planning the first 10, I handed off the reins. Keith Rice, who is featured throughout these pages, quickly targeted Mount Washington for the group. On May 20, eight of us went up the Ammonoosuc Ravine Trail and ran into a nice jolt of winter weather (snow, wind, fog) outside the Lakes of the Clouds Hut. Visibility quickly became brutal. Shortly after leaving the hut, we missed the left turn for the Crawford Path and had to double back. In addition, two members of our team did not have the proper footwear and another had fallen during the ascent near the Ammonoosuc Falls. I remember cramping near the top, but I was packing a pocketful of deli ham to combat it. All that adventure aside, we made the summit fairly clean and got some decent photos.

Washington 2006

However, there were just five of us on the return hike down the Gulfside Trail to the Jewell Trail. The other three, which included the pair lacking boots, soon became known affectionately as "The Cocoa Trio." They took the Cog Railway down to start making dinner back at our Old Cherry Mountain Road campsite in Carroll. Of course, The Cocoa Trio (yes, they sipped cocoa on the train) got one more look at us where the railway tracks and Gulfside Trail intersected. Well, they got a nice look at the moon…a few of them.

There were also a pair of trips out west with my wife Carrie, to Colorado in 1999 and Utah in 2000. These featured some hiking, albeit a bit lighter, in Rocky Mountain National Park, Zion National Park, and Bryce Canyon National Park. Along with multiple ascents of Massachusetts' highest point, Mount Greylock (3,491 feet), as well as southern New Hampshire's biggest mountain, Mount Monadnock (3,166 feet), I was getting out pretty well since returning to New England from Virginia in the summer of 1998.

It was, in fact, my three-plus years of living in Richmond, Virginia, that I began to develop into an actual hiker. During that time (1995 to 1998), I got into a nice groove of alternating my weekends between traveling north to Boston to visit Carrie, whom I married in November 1998, and traveling west to hike in Shenandoah National Park (SNP). I churned out a lot of miles in SNP, and one of its real charms is that many of its trailheads are located along Skyline Drive, the 105-mile scenic road that runs the crest of the Blue Ridge Mountains.

So, while the SNP hikes often featured summits of 3,000 to 4,000 feet including Hawksbill, Stony Man, Old Rag, and Bearfence, the trailheads were often only a few hundred feet below. It made for an interesting training ground for New Hampshire's White Mountains. In short, SNP taught me the value and joy of the big summit view. That "the juice was worth the squeeze" and that not all miles were created equal. Something that I learned again the hard way years later in the Whites. For example, hiking the 2.5 miles between the Garfield Shelter and Galehead Hut can be a challenging and dangerous two-plus hour grind, while the 2.5 miles leaving the Lincoln Woods Trailhead can be done without breaking a sweat in under an hour.

Virginia also delivered in the wildlife category for me in ways the Whites have not. I had five black-bear experiences in those three years of hiking SNP and a few of them were up close and personal. Once, while hiking across a below-treeline ridge, on a slightly downward slope, I heard the unmistakable sound of branches breaking. I stopped. I looked quickly in all directions. Nothing. I started moving again and, *snap, snap, snap*. I stopped. This time it had been louder, yet a much more deliberate 360-degree look came up empty. I started to hike again and, *crack*. Instead of looking around, this time I looked up. Straight up. And there it was. The rump of a small black bear rapidly descending from a tree and breaking off branches on the way down. *Crack. Crack. Crack.*

I walked backwards up the trail with a purpose. As the spooked bear landed on the ground directly in front of me, I was still moving backwards. Thankfully, it went in the opposite direction. For the next mile or so of trail, I experienced huge adrenaline surges wondering if the black bear was done with me.

As for my actual introduction to hiking, it dates back to my college days. In November of 1985, I was 18 years old and a freshman at Fitchburg State College in Fitchburg, Massachusetts. Located in the north-central part of the state and less than a half-hour from the New Hampshire border, Fitchburg was a dump of a municipality in the mid-1980s. An old mill/manufacturing city that peaked around 1900, Fitchburg was dirty, tough, and poor.

A few years later, I drove a city cab on the overnight shift, 6pm to 6am. My best customers were the crack dealers who relocated to Fitchburg from New York, as they would pay me to shuttle local girls to their parties and themselves around town peddling product. Eventually, they'd need me to get them to a hotel in Leominster, Fitchburg's Twin City. They liked me and called me "Taximan." With the exception of hearing a few gunshots one night while waiting on a pick-up outside their party house, and the occasional firearms sighting in the car, they weren't a problem.

While registering for Fitchburg State's 1986 spring semester, I spotted the one-credit elective "Intro to Mountain Hiking." I thought it was cool that I could earn a credit for a course like that. Plus, at the same moment, I was genuinely interested in the subject. My early childhood had included a good amount of family camping and outdoor play. I grew up on the west side of Holliston, Massachusetts, just a few miles from the start of the Boston Marathon and Interstate 495. I have some faint family memories of climbing Mount Monadnock as a kid as well as trekking around White Mountains-area attractions such as Lost River Gorge, The Flume, and Polar Caves. I signed up for the course.

Intro to Mountain Hiking featured one hour of classroom discussion each week. Attendance was mandatory and directly affected your grade. There was just one paper to write and, at the end of the semester, an eight-mile hike along the Wapack Trail in southern New Hampshire that included summiting Mount Watatic (1,832 feet). The course was great. I looked forward to each week's lesson and discussion, which ranged from gear and map reading to understanding weather at higher altitudes and elevation gain. So much so, I didn't miss a class the entire semester. As the class hike grew closer, I learned that it was on the same day as Fitchburg State's infamous Fubar Keg Races.

As a college freshman, I had never experienced the keg races, but I had heard some stories. I was torn. But I soon learned that the hike was mandatory. Skip the hike, fail the course. So, I motored through the eight miles (I was 18) and made sure I was part of the first wave of students back to campus. The hike itself was fine. I didn't find anything special that day, on the trail or inside myself. But it was enjoyable. Not as fun as watching the keg races. Those were magical—teams of five racing to finish a quarter barrel of bad yellow beer with a complex set of rules and procedures that included penalty beers. Awesome.

Having attended every class and participated in the eight-mile hike along the Wapack Trail, I calculated I had a B in Intro to Mountain Hiking. At

Fitchburg State, that was a 3.0 and good enough for me. So I blew off the one paper assigned to us. Well, turns out the paper, too, was mandatory. I flunked the class.

I would go on to flunk 13 other classes at Fitchburg State before finally graduating in 1993. I finished with a 2.52 grade-point average and a bachelor of science degree in Communications Media with a concentration in technical writing/journalism. But that's a different college story. In this one, I go on to camp in Shenandoah National Park during spring break 1990 and hike in Great Smoky Mountains National Park during spring break 1991. The latter trip included seeing the Grateful Dead in Washington, D.C., and summiting Tennessee's Mount LeConte (6,593 feet), the sixth tallest mountain east of the Mississippi River. It was on the Mount LeConte hike that I recall thinking repeatedly, and saying aloud a few times, "This might be the greatest thing I've ever done." I believe it was this day, the Mount LeConte trek in March of 1991, that launched my life as a hiker.

While I have no proof, I do believe I am the only person to have completed the New Hampshire 48, the New England 67*, and the New England Hundred Highest^ who has also flunked Intro to Mountain Hiking at the university level. For the record, I did re-take the course one year later with the same professor. On the first day of class, students were asked if we had ever hiked in the area. I raised my hand and said, "I hiked eight miles along the Wapack Trail~ last spring and climbed Mount Watatic." The professor replied, "That's the same hike we will do in this course." I said, "I know. I did it with you last semester but you flunked me for not writing the paper."

This time I wrote the paper, but, once again, the hike was scheduled on the same day as the Fubar Keg Races. I took my chances and blew off the hike. I got a 3.5.

---

*The New England 67 comprises the New Hampshire 48 plus 14 mountains in Maine and five mountains in Vermont recognized by the AMC as measuring 4,000 feet or higher.
^ The New England Hundred Highest comprises the 100 tallest mountains in New England as recognized by the AMC and includes 59 total peaks in New Hampshire, 27 in Maine, and 14 in Vermont.
~ The Wapack Trail is 21.5 miles and stretches from North Pack Monadnock Mountain in Greenfield, New Hampshire, to Mount Watatic in Ashburnham, Massachusetts. On December 4, 2016, I day-hiked the entire Wapack Trail with two hiking partners featured in this book, Eric Engler and Jason Unger. We trekked southbound and the post-hike meal that night was not so glamorous (see McDonald's, Jaffrey, NH).

# 2012
# FRESHMAN YEAR
# PEAKS #2-8

# CHAPTER 1
# Finding the Magic

Date: Friday, May 18, 2012
Mountain Range: Franconia
Peaks/Elevation (feet): Lafayette 5,260, Lincoln 5,089
Route (Loop): Old Bridle Path to Greenleaf to Franconia
   Ridge to Falling Waters
Total Distance: 9 miles
Hiking Partners: Eric Hanson, Keith Rice
Road to 48: #2, #3

By April of 2012, I had read and re-read *Backpacker* magazine's description of the Franconia Ridge so often that I became obsessed with hiking it. That spring, I just kept replaying the phrase *"Get a taste of the Alps"* in my head. So much so, that when it came time to finalize my annual weekend-before-Memorial-Day trip with college buddies, I knew it would be this hike.

I also knew this was a bit of a selfish decision. Something not done before in planning the previous 16 Outdoor Adventures. Launched in May 1996 from my apartment in Richmond, Virginia, the Outdoor Adventure (OA) was a rocket ship of a weekend. It started with eight friends who met in the late 1980s/early '90s on the university streets of Fitchburg, Massachusetts, and grew to double digits by Year 3. In its first decade, OA weekends were Thursday-through-Monday marathons. Each year's adventure was highlighted by a hike of some significance—big mileage, summit, waterfall, etc. Previous trips included hiking in Shenandoah National Park as well as summiting the highest points in Maine, New Hampshire, Vermont, Massachusetts, and Connecticut.

However, starting in 2008, attendance began to suffer due to the traditional lifecycle challenges of work, wives, kids, mortgages, and vacation time. After a decade-long run of never having more than one invitee miss a trip, we had four opt out of OA 13. This happened again in 2009 and 2010. In 2011, there were just three of us on the OA

16 hike, which featured Tuckerman Ravine and its Lunch Rocks. This pattern fueled my decision to target the Franconia Ridge Loop in May 2012. And while I had no knowledge of the New Hampshire 48 at the time, it was this decision that changed the course of the next 10 years of my life.

Eric Hanson, Keith Rice, and I assembled at the Lafayette Place parking area off I-93 North on Friday morning, May 18. While there was just three of us for the OA 17 hike, that was fine. There was an air of anticipation about the adventure as I was ultra-confident it would live up to the hype. In short, I was salivating for that *"taste of the Alps"* as we geared up and stretched out. I was also excited to debut my first hiking-specific gear purchase, the Gregory Z55 backpack. Why that pack? Well, *Backpacker* magazine named it the 2010 best "all-around" pack and, at that time, that was good enough for me. It didn't take long to realize that a 55-liter pack was too much pack for a day hike (it weighs 3.7 pounds). Growing pains.

"The weather was perfect," said Hanson. "There was little to no wind. The sun was out. It was warm."

We had agreed to go up the Old Bridle Path to the Greenleaf Hut and summit Lafayette first. It was a group decision led by Hanson, who was familiar with the hike. This is not the direction of a traditional Franconia Ridge Loop as ascending Falling Waters is the safer, more popular, and easier-to-navigate route. In fact, descending Falling Waters is a bitch on the knees, and it's especially dangerous when wet or icy. However, to this day, having hiked this loop in both directions multiple times, as well as during all four seasons, I prefer climbing Lafayette first. The views of the ridge going up are outstanding and a real sense of anticipation builds on the climb. Plus, hiking down the ridge as it gradually declines, especially from Lincoln to Little Haystack, is uniquely special.

"I had done the loop three or four times before," said Hanson. "This hike was just after the Sharon years. My ex-wife. I hadn't been hiking at the time like I was before I met her. It was a relationship that kept me away from the mountains. I had forgotten how awesome it was to be in the Whites, especially when you get a day like we got that day. So it was sort of a return for me and there were a lot of feelings coming back on the trip."

As we went up the Old Bridle Path and got a bunch of good looks at our destination, excitement grew. It was happening. We were finally on the Franconia Ridge Loop. As we neared the Greenleaf Hut, I felt I could reach out and touch the summits of both Lafayette and Lincoln. However, I could see that Rice was uncharacteristically struggling.

"I was completely gassed when we hit the Greenleaf Hut. I had already dipped into my chocolate reserve just to get there. It's a simple hiker trick. You pack energy food, Snickers, Kit Kats, whatever. Quick sugar bursts to get you moving," said Rice. "But I was in the worst shape of my life then, 2012. Not only was I gassed, but I knew I was carrying too much weight. That's not where I ever wanted to be."

The Greenleaf Hut is 2.9 miles from the parking lot and it sits at an elevation of 4,200 feet. We fueled up here, on both food and water. We also cooled down and got about a half hour of rest while taking in the ridge view. It was an ideal stop on what was becoming a bluebird day.

Hanson and Rice at the Greenleaf Hut

"Just after Greenleaf, there was a difference in my gait and step," Rice said. "The stop was key for me. Refueled, and with some sustenance in my gut, the shakiness in my step went away."

The three of us hit our stride climbing the final 1.1 miles to the summit of Lafayette. The 1,000 feet of vertical gain wasn't a problem, and we celebrated the hike's highest point by taking a round of photos and capturing some video.

"It was so beautiful up there. We got that special 360 view from the summit," said Hanson. "But it was windy. You can really hear it whipping on the video we shot. At one point, it was hard to hear our own voices."

Me and Keith Rice

Looking down the ridge, at those 1.7 miles to Lincoln and Little Haystack, there was not only a sense of satisfaction but also a natural feeling of accomplishment. We set out for Lincoln, just .9 miles away, and targeted it as our lunch spot. We knew we wanted to soak up as much of the view, the sun, and the day as we could.

"It was gorgeous that day. Everywhere we looked. Everything to the east, seeing into Vermont to the west, and Canada to the north. Unobstructed view of thousands of peaks," said Rice. "We were on top of it. We were in it, and it was all around us. And we knew how special it was in that moment."

As we worked our way down to Little Haystack (4,760 feet), we separated a bit. Each of us finding some alone time on the trail. It just happened organically.

"We spread out on the ridge," said Rice. "Not intentionally. We were hiking our own hike. We all got into our pace."

"The descent down the ridge, heading for Little Haystack. I remember that being the magical part," said Hanson.

It was during this stretch, on the gradual sloping decline of .7 miles between Lincoln and Little Haystack, that I had my moment with the Whites. I was moving smoothly, freely as one does after a nice meal and a few cold beverages at 5,000 feet. Maybe it was an epiphany. Maybe it was the realization of completing a personal goal set some two months earlier with the reading of a magazine article. In short, I finally got my *"taste of the Alps"* and I liked it every bit of it.

Rice and Hanson on the ridge

"Everything that day was just so perfect along the ridge," said Hanson.

When we reached Little Haystack, the three of us reassembled. Before heading down the Falling Waters Trail, we took inventory of our supplies as well as each other. We had six miles behind us, and three remaining to get back to the trailhead. Of course, the final three miles included a drop in elevation of nearly 3,000 feet and we knew the trail would be wet. The Falling Waters Trail, as evidenced by its name, features a series of cascades that, while insanely stunning, is very dangerous. The trail zigzags across the falling water on multiple occasions.

Hanson on the Falling Waters Trail

At one point on the top portion, I lost my footing and began to descend a bit too quickly. I was rock hopping and nearly out of control. I was able to stop short on a large granite plateau, but in doing so, momentum carried my upper body forward. I bent at the waist in an effort to gather myself but my backpack came over the top of my head. Ugh. I didn't have my waist strap buckled. Freshman move. This carried me off the plateau and into runaway-train mode. It was not good. I was scared. I had to throw myself off the trail and into a group of small trees to bring me to a halt. I was fortunate to not get hurt. Lesson learned.

Around this same time, another member of our hiking party was seemingly starting to struggle a bit.

"We were worried about Hanson," said Rice. "He was lagging behind at times going down Falling Waters. We kept stopping and waiting for him. One time we really were concerned for him and

6

waited it out for a while. I knew it could be a treacherous route down. It's just so steep."

Hanson admitted he was taking it slow and not focused on making good time.

"I was wearing camping clothes. I had a flannel work shirt on, baseball cap, and sunglasses. Just taking it slow," said Hanson. "And I was relishing being on trail again."

While Rice and I were genuinely concerned, we had been hiking with Hanson for 20 years. We knew each other pretty well at this point. Thus, our worry was for all the right reasons and at the proper level. We also knew not to truly separate on trail, or, in this case, allow too much space between us.

"Now, again, we all hike our own hike and he was fine," said Rice. "But we were worried and would wait for him. Just making sure he was all right. He was a different dude on the way down, quiet and slow, than on the way up. But he'd come along smiling and always be okay."

The three of us returned to the cars safely to find four of our Fitchburg State friends waiting for us in the parking lot. Although it was part of the OA weekend plan, it was nice to see them after a day on trail. We played a little whiffle ball and had a beverage in the parking lot before heading to our Old Cherry Mountain Road campsite in Carroll. The same area, but a different site than our group stayed at during our Mount Washington trip six years earlier. We also shared our Franconia Ridge Loop experience.

"It was a great hike," said Rice. "Perfect conditions on top, which you don't get every time. So when you get them, you savor them."

"You couldn't be in a better spot than the Franconia Ridge on a day like that," said Hanson. "Those peaks. The 360 view. That's the magic."

## CLIFF NOTES: WMS CHAPTER 1

🏃 Always keep an eye on your hiking partners regardless of their level of experience or expertise.

🏃 Store high-energy snacks, like chocolate bars or trail mix, where they can be accessed while on the move.

🏃 Match your backpack size to the size and needs of your hike.

---

**Facebook Post:**

Keith Gentili
May 30, 2012

FRANCONIA RIDGE TRAIL, NH—While the audio on this ain't great especially when the wind picks up at the edge, so ignore it, here's a nice look from NH's 6th & 7th highest peaks (Mt. Lafayette & Lincoln) featuring great 360 views. I shot this last weekend for the kids but it's worth a look if summit views interest you. Great loop trail, about 9 miles total including 1.7 of pure ridge (i.e. the back of a stegosaurus), with three nice peaks and three big waterfalls on way down.

# CHAPTER 2
# Discovering the Risk

Date: Sunday, August 12, 2012
Mountain Range: Franconia
Peaks/Elevation (feet): Flume 4,328, Liberty 4,459
Route (Loop): Whitehouse to Flume Slide to Franconia Ridge to
  Liberty Springs to Whitehouse
Total Distance: 10.1 miles
Hiking Partners: Eric Hanson, Hannah Sparks, Eric Engler
Road to 48: #4, #5

The adrenaline from the May 18 hike of the Franconia Ridge Loop stayed with me all through June and into July. It was at an afternoon family barbecue on July 4, 2012, in New Boston, NH, following the town's award-winning parade that I first heard the words "New Hampshire 48." They came from New Boston resident Brad Bingham, who just threw them at me in a sort of off-the-cuff remark as I was detailing my adventure summiting Mount Lafayette and Mount Lincoln.

"My uncle climbed the New Hampshire 48," said Bingham. "You should do that."

The rest of the party was a blur. I needed to find out more about the New Hampshire 48 and fast. Bingham provided a few more of the basic details (climb all 48 mountains in the Whites recognized by the Appalachian Mountain Club, all 4,000 feet or higher, and get some sort of diploma), but, to his credit, he left me wanting more. A few hours later, I had my wife Carrie and our daughters Julia and Sarah in the car headed for home. That night, I dug in. Even in 2012, there were plenty of websites, online maps, and resources to read through. My research continued all through July as I began to put together the plan that carried me for the next four years to "graduation."

It started with the single goal of completing the New Hampshire 48 (NH 48) on or just before my 48th birthday, which was September 27, 2015. That meant I had three years and two months to climb the remaining 45 peaks on the list. At this time, I believed the hiking season was only six months long, from April to October. Why? Well, I had climbed both Mount Washington and the Franconia Ridge Loop in May and figured November was simply too cold and snowy to "hike" mountains. After spending far too many nights breaking down routes and trails, and learning all I could about the NH 48, I determined that one hike a month would be enough to put me in position to complete my goal. My first two official bookstore purchases that helped me formulate this plan were the 1997 book *Hiker's Guide to the Mountains of New Hampshire* by Jared Gange and the Exploring New Hampshire's White Mountains Waterproof TOPO Map & Guide. Now, I just had to get started.

I targeted Mount Flume and Mount Liberty next. It just made sense to me to complete the peaks along the Franconia Ridge. I knew it was special on that ridge and the idea of getting back on it was motivating. In fact, I decided to focus specifically on mountains in the Franconia Notch for the remainder of the 2012 hiking season. The Kinsmans and Moosilauke would follow. I felt this would make me a sort of expert on the area before moving on to whatever would be next; that decision could wait until the spring of 2013. So, invitations went out to my hiking friends for an August 12 climb of Flume and Liberty.

The route would be steep as my plan was to ascend the Flume Slide Trail. This trail's final 1.5 miles gain 2,000 feet as hikers make their way from an elevation of 2,300 to the Flume summit of 4,328. I learned quickly that 1,000 feet of elevation gain over one mile of trail was steep. Well, this was steeper than that, and that made it attractive. This was also part of the original plan, to always take the most challenging and, ultimately, rewarding trail to the summit. I knew I would want the most bang for the buck every time out, mostly because I thought I might only climb each mountain once. Thus, I better get it right.

Eric Hanson got back to me immediately saying he was in and that his girlfriend Hannah would be joining us. This was great news, as a piece of me was not sure anyone would be coming along on this trip, or any part of the NH 48 ride. Hanson and Hannah were in love and would be great company.

"We were in the first years of knowing each other. She was a carpenter. She was jacked, totally fit, and totally kickass," said Hanson of the woman he would soon marry and build a family with. "That hike was where Team Hannahson originated. It was born that day."

Team Hannahson

Eric Engler tagged the couple "Team Hannahson" as we were preparing our gear at the northern end of the Flume Gorge parking lot off I-93 North (Hannah + Hanson = Hannahson). Engler, too, agreed to come on the hike despite having limited experience on trail.

"I liked hanging out with you guys and I do remember being asked to go on the Liberty-Flume hike and not really understanding what the scope of it was," said Engler, who grew up in the beach community of Westerly, Rhode Island. "I didn't have much hiking experience. I went on the OA hikes but that was it. [Keith] Rice was always into hiking and outdoor stuff and Hanson had been hiking since he was younger. That kind of thing just wasn't on my plate. It was never on my radar. Not in a bad way. It's just I never went camping or hiking as a kid. I never went boating. I skied once when I was 14. So, I didn't have that background."

Rice, who was on the Franconia Ridge Loop hike, was unable to join us for Flume and Liberty. Hanson, Hannah, Engler, and I strapped on our packs and headed out. By now, I had read so much about the Flume Slide Trail that I felt I knew what to expect. Hanson, however, had real experience.

"I had already done Flume Slide, up and down, and in the rain— exactly how you are not supposed to do it," said Hanson. "The last time I did it, which was a long time ago, I remember seeing a guy who fell and was bloodied."

Hanson shared part of that story with us as we made our way up the Liberty Springs Trail discussing the upcoming steepness of the Flume Slide. It was a double-edged sword as it was nice to hear he was familiar with the trail. But, hearing the trail had a casualty, well, it confirmed the risk. Engler recalled that.

"I remember Hanson saying something about the guy who fell on Flume years ago that was bloodied," said Engler. "That stuck with me."

Hanson remembered one thing about Engler that day.

"Engler had terrible boots," said Hanson. "We had a steep climb ahead of us up that slide and he had work boots on."

At the 1.4-mile mark, our group departed the Liberty Springs Trail and turned right onto the Flume Slide Trail, which starts out gradually and continues to climb like that for a while. We hadn't seen any other hikers at this point on trail, which was not surprising due to the day's weather, which held a chance of showers. But as we began to approach the bottom of the slide, about three miles from the parking lot, we noticed some folks approaching us. One of the hikers was limping, moving both slowly and cautiously. As we neared each other, he was obviously injured. We could see that he was bleeding.

"We saw him on the approach, literally at the base of the slide," said Hanson. "It was like, oh man, the same thing is happening again as this was exactly where the other guy was that I saw years earlier."

The hiker told us he fell coming down the Flume Slide, tumbling and sliding a bit before coming to a stop. He was in pain and had the open wounds to prove it. However, his hiking partners were fine and confident they would be able to return to the parking lot safely. Although the situation was controlled, it was apparent that it was still a situation.

"He was a bloody mess. Knees, elbow, it was like a full-body bleed. But nothing on the head," said Hanson. "He was totally defeated though, just as the first guy was."

As we parted ways and both groups moved in their destination's direction, Hanson began to share more from his original encounter many years earlier.

"I walked up to him, he was covered in blood, and I said, 'Are you all right, man?' He said, 'Yeah, I'm all right.' I asked again, 'Are you sure?' Then, he said, 'You shouldn't go up there,' but I was training for Mount Rainier and was like, 'I'll be fine.'"

Hanson summited Flume without issue that day just as we did on this hike. We navigated our way up the slide safely, utilizing routes on and adjacent to the slide.

"We had no problems that day at all. We monkeyed our way up," said Hanson, who did indeed climb Mount Rainier in September of 2001. "Back then, I had the most experience of our group in the Whites. I had done about half of the 48 including this trail. I felt we'd be fine."

We had lunch on the summit. Views were a bit limited as clouds were prevalent. After an hour or so on top of Flume, we began our 1.2-mile trek over to Liberty via the Franconia Ridge Trail. There's some nice rock scrambling through this stretch as well as a bit of a drop in elevation, as we bottomed out at 3,900 feet. Then, we climbed up Liberty to its summit (4,459 feet), a wide-open space with wonderful panoramic views of Franconia Notch and beyond. On the final ascent, I kept singing the chorus to the Grateful Dead song "Liberty."

*Ooo, freedom.*

*Ooo, liberty.*

*Oh, leave me alone.*

*To find my own way home.*

*I'm gonna find my own way home.*

It's a song from the band's final batch of tunes in the early 1990s. Robert Hunter wrote the lyrics. Jerry Garcia put it to music and sang it. While it didn't appear on a studio album, the band played "Liberty" live 57 times between 1993 and 1995. It's on the gotta-have box set "So Many Roads (1965-1995)." I first saw the Grateful Dead in 1987 and remain on the bus today. I saw Garcia take the stage 20 times before he died on August 9, 1995. My final Grateful Dead concert was June 15, 1995, in Highgate, Vermont, at the Franklin County Airport. "Liberty" was the encore that night and the last song I ever saw Jerry Garcia perform.

On our descent from the Liberty summit, we stopped at the Liberty Springs Campsite and had a nice chat with a ranger. We learned a little about the site's rules, regulations, and some of the trail work and restoration that was going on in the area. All that was left was the nearly three-mile trek down to the trailhead and the car.

"I always remember going down Liberty because it's such an arduous staircase down," said Hanson. "That's how I think of Liberty. A relentless staircase."

**CLIFF NOTES: WMS CHAPTER 2**

- Always check on fellow hikers with injuries you see on the trail. They may be concussed or have injuries worse than they realize.
- Set hiking goals, of any level of difficulty, to fuel long-term engagement and enthusiasm.
- Assess on-trail situations, and hiking conditions, slowly while considering all members of your group.
- Wear proper footwear every time out.

---

**Facebook Post:**

Keith Gentili
August 13, 2012

MT. FLUME (4,328)—The view at the conclusion of the tough Flume Slide Trail which was part of yesterday's Mt. Flume/ Liberty loop that included a vertical gain of 3,700 feet and 10 total miles. Liberty, at 4,459, is NH's 18th highest peak. Note to locals, Flume Slide Trail is not safe for children. Too steep, too long, too wet and too much loose rock and large granite slabs all add up to too many white-knuckle moments.

# CHAPTER 3
## Grasping the Scope

Date: Sunday, September 23, 2012
Mountain Range: Kinsman
Peaks/Elevation (feet): North Kinsman 4,293, South Kinsman 4,358
Route (Out and Back): Lonesome Lake to Cascade Brook to Fishin' Jimmy to Kinsman Ridge
Total Distance: 11 miles
Hiking Partner: Eric Engler
Road to 48: #6, #7

The Flume-Liberty hike helped confirm what I had hoped, that the pursuit of the NH 48 would serve me well. For starters, hiking once a month was simply healthy. I was working on getting in shape in 2012; I was running a few times a week, and it paired nicely with regular hiking trips. While not fully consumed by the 48 quest, I was continuing to read and research hike after hike. I had an unquenchable thirst for all things New Hampshire 4,000-footer during those first few months. I knew I wanted to inspire others to join me, and I believed being somewhat of an authority on the subject matter would only help. In some ways, I felt like I was selling, or at least marketing, the NH 48 to others…and that really meant to three people in particular.

At this point, I was confident that Eric Hanson was in. His enthusiasm for being back in the Whites was unmistakable that summer. He was also on record stating if he were to fully pursue the 48, he would hike all of them again, essentially starting with our Franconia Ridge Loop hike. However, as I targeted North Kinsman and South Kinsman for my September hike, Hanson chose to pass. Keith Rice, whom I considered a prime candidate to come along for the entire NH 48 ride, also passed on this trip and shared that he was not setting his sights on the larger goal either. Rice would often remind me in 2012, "The 48 is your thing."

Then Eric Engler signed on for what I was framing in my head as my birthday hike; September 23 was a Sunday and I would be turning 45 on September 27 (that Thursday). It was a bit surprising to me as Engler was pretty clear about his thoughts on hiking the Whites. The Kinsmans trek would be another test as it mixed vertical gain with distance.

"I wasn't interested in the area but I appreciated it very much. I just didn't have the resources to research the trail, but I trusted you," Engler told me. "You were inspirational. You got us guys out there. But I was raw, super raw. That's how I look at it. You call it 'Freshman Year' and I agree. Even later, as I look at the pictures, I see how ill prepared I may have been for those early hikes. I didn't have the right gear or even a first-aid kit. But you were going for another hike and I wanted to go."

While Engler admits to not being interested in the White Mountains as an area, he did have some family history with it. And it was part of his story as he reflected on hiking the 48, and more specifically the mountains in Franconia Notch.

"When we were younger, my wife Kelli and I would drive around the Whites and we'd see the ridges and mountains from the highway. We'd think they are just so big," said Engler. "So, when we were driving through Franconia Notch, and these mountains are being split by the highway, we'd look up and I never knew the names of any of them. My family has driven through there so many times and I had seen them, and now, I was on them. And they are as huge as we thought."

In fact, Engler credits his wife and family for supporting his chase of the 48. He notes that the timing was right for him to take on this type of personal endeavor.

"My kids were 10 and 12 in 2012. They were not babies anymore. So, I did have more opportunities to go hiking and hang with the dudes," said Engler. "My wife didn't have any problems with that. And as those early hikes went on, she never had a problem with it. I'm thankful for that. Because it was a lot, especially with the drive back and forth. The logistics of the trip and getting the most bang for the buck as we were doing then."

Engler traveled from his home in north-central Massachusetts that Sunday morning and met me at my place in New Boston. We weren't early risers and that was never part of my hiking formula anyway. I have always preferred sunset to sunrise and believed strongly in hiking down the mountain during the evening's Golden Hour, that last hour of daylight. There was always less folks out on the trail and the stillness of the evening had a way of seducing me every time out. I can blame it on the sky. I drove us that day from New Boston to the notch in my 2004 Honda Accord and we parked at the south end of the Lafayette Place Campground off I-93 South.

The Lonesome Lake Trail starts right there in the parking lot at an elevation of 1,770 feet and ascends between the campground loops. We were still adjusting our packs as we passed a few fall campers taking down their tents. It is just 1.2 miles to Lonesome Lake but that part of the trail climbs nearly 1,000 feet to 2,740, making it early vertical gain. We took a left at the junction onto the Cascade Brook Trail and followed it around the lake to the Fishin' Jimmy Trail. We passed the Lonesome Lake Hut. Then, for the next two miles, we climbed, making our way up the west side of the Kinsman Ridge.

Just .2 miles before reaching the top of the ridge sits Kinsman Pond and the Kinsman Pond Shelter. Engler and I agreed to push forward but we made a pact to return to the pond to soak our sure-to-be-sore feet on the way down. It was a great decision and motivated us through the remainder of our climb, as well as the 1.3-mile hike south along the ridge to peak bag both of the Kinsmans. The summit of North Kinsman is just .4 miles from the intersection of the Fishin'

Jimmy Trail and Kinsman Ridge Trail. It delivers great views east, across I-93, of the Franconia Ridge.

"The view from the north summit, across the highway to the Franconia Ridge, as well as Liberty and Flume, confirmed for me just how big these mountains were and how much of an effort it took to get up there," said Engler.

We worked our way further south, .9 miles, to the summit of South Kinsman. There are a few lookouts there with the best views at the southern knob. We chose to return to North Kinsman to have our lunch and rest up before descending. All the while, we continued to set our sights on Kinsman Pond. But it was that view of the Franconia Ridge, from North Kinsman, that really put the entire notch in perspective for me. Having now been atop the two ridges (Kinsman and Franconia) and having hiked the terrain between each and I-93, I had an understanding of Franconia Notch that I never got from driving through it during the last 15 years. I also felt the NH 48 puzzle at work, how the combination of the hikes and peaks fit together to deliver an outdoor education specific to the region. My NH 48 journey was only at 7/48, but I really was on my way.

Lonesome Lake and the Franconia Ridge

The two of us wrapped up lunch and began our return descent to Kinsman Pond. We stopped at the "new" shelter, which was built in 2007. The original was built in 1966 and replaced by this one, which still had a real shine on it. We then found our way to the water, something we had talked about since first passing the pond on our climb up. We took our boots off, and finally got our feet wet.

"It was so beautiful," said Engler. "I remember walking right up to the edge of the pond. It was absolutely beautiful that day."

We enjoyed the quiet solitude of the pond while our feet soaked. I was able to find a rock to stand on just a few feet from the pond's edge where we were sitting. At that same moment, the sun began to duck behind the ridge. As I stood there, taking in the view of the Kinsman Ridge, Engler took a picture. To this day, it remains one of my favorite images captured during the entire NH 48. I am just drawn to the mixed imagery and juxtaposition of the water and the mountains.

"We had climbed Mount Washington for OA 11, and I'd seen the Lakes of the Clouds. But other than that, I had never really experienced ponds or lakes while hiking in the mountains," said Engler. "It just didn't make sense to me. I was surprised to see the pond up there and it was so beautiful."

21

The return from Kinsman Pond included one final stop at Lonesome Lake, which included a pop-in at the Lonesome Lake Hut. Another special spot in the Whites, Lonesome Lake Hut also provides just a spectacular view of the Franconia Ridge and specifically Mount Lafayette. Whether you sit along the west shore, or sit in the hut while fueling up, drying out, or warming up, the view across the lake to the Franconia Ridge alone is worth the 1.5-mile hike from the Lafayette Place Campground parking lot.

Engler and I made the final trek to the trailhead as the evening began to set in. Being a Sunday night, and both of us needing to work in the morning, our energy was focused on finishing up and getting home. As we made our final strides through the campground, it was quiet. We didn't see anybody else and my car sat alone in the parking lot. I instantly liked that feeling of being the last ones off the mountain. This was the first time it was clear to me that we were, indeed, the last ones off the trail, but it was something I would repeat—purposely—many more times on my NH 48 journey. I remember when Engler finally settled into my Accord and I started the engine, his six-foot frame just melted into his seat.

"Dude, that was a big hike," he said. "I'm beat. That was a really big hike."

**CLIFF NOTES: WMS CHAPTER 3**

🚶 Work to develop unconditional trust with your hiking partners while on trail as they will heighten the overall experience.

🚶 Build time into each hike to explore something not in your original plan such as a pond or waterfall.

🚶 Trailheads located at campgrounds offer an ideal option for an overnight stay, especially after a long hike.

**Facebook Post:**

Keith Gentili
September 24, 2012

KINSMAN POND—Nestled up to the base of North Kinsman is Kinsman Pond and we hit it on the way back down near sunset. The total hike was about 11 miles, 8 ½ hours, and 3,400 feet of vert. And two peaks closer to becoming a 48er...

# CHAPTER 4
# The Fitchburg State Hiking Club

Date: Sunday, October 21, 2012
Mountain Range: Kinsman
Peak/Elevation (feet): Moosilauke 4,802
Route (Out and Back): Beaver Brook to Benton
Total Distance: 7.6 miles
Hiking Partners: Eric Hanson, Eric Engler, Keith Rice
Road to 48: #8

As I began planning my final hike of 2012, I knew it had to be Mount Moosilauke. That would leave just Cannon Mountain as the remaining peak in Franconia Notch. Moosilauke was the choice for a couple of reasons. One, I really didn't know what it looked like...as opposed to Cannon, which I've been staring up at my entire adult life while driving through the notch. Two, I kept reading about how its summit was both massive and bald, which was a real draw. And three, the Beaver Brook Trail is listed in Jared Gange's *Hiker's Guide to the Mountains of New Hampshire* as a Classic Hike of the White Mountains. Here's the description taken from the book that sold me. *"From wild and beautiful Kinsman Notch, steep Beaver Brook Trail works its way up past a series of rushing cascades, often using iron rungs and stone steps. This is a long but rewarding route to Moosilauke's mighty summit and its far-reaching views."*

Yep, it was definitely going to be Moosilauke before breaking for the winter. I also knew I wanted to pull together all the folks who joined me on the previous hikes in launching the pursuit of the NH 48. It just felt right, that as the season was coming to a close, we all get together for a final adventure. Moosilauke and the Beaver Brook Trail was ideal, thanks to its southern location and proximity to I-93. Plus, the promise of cascades, iron rungs, and a massive bald summit made it very appealing. The invitations went out to my three fellow Fitchburg State graduates: Eric Hanson, Eric Engler, and Keith Rice. And, for the first time on my 48 quest, all invited parties accepted. It was on.

25

"It was like the Fellowship of the Ring," said Hanson. "We were all going to band together and do this."

Knowing Hanson was on board for this hike, and all that lay ahead in the following years, was a major ingredient in my early NH 48 success on trail, as well as in my confidence in choosing routes. We were college roommates during our senior year of 1991-1992 and remained close ever since. Hanson brought experience and enthusiasm to the trail that balanced out my preparation and sometimes cautious approach. In short, he liked to get after it and that was good for me.

"I was all in by that point," Hanson told me. "You said, 'I'm doing it. Come with me.' And I'm sitting here thinking, 'Yeah, I'm doing it with you. I'm totally in.'"

Hanson, Engler, Rice and I met Sunday, October 21, 2012, at the Beaver Brook Trailhead (elevation 1,870 feet) off Route 112 in Kinsman Notch. We each drove separately and our four cars were scattered about the parking area. Hanson came from Massachusetts' North Shore while Rice made the trek from his home on the South Shore. We gathered to say our hellos and dispersed to finish preparing our packs and bodies for the climb. Similar to the feeling at the start of the Franconia Ridge Loop, there was anticipation in the air.

"That was the day. I'm looking at these other three guys and thinking we would all do it," said Hanson in regard to the NH 48. "I named it the Fitchburg State Hiking Club right there. It was a joke, but it stuck. We got these four guys and we are going to climb these 48 mountains. Moosilauke is where it really started."

Engler, as always, was happy to be on board for a hike and among his college friends. He knew he would enjoy the day but he never made any promises for the future.

"When I started hiking some of the 48 that first year," said Engler, "I did think, 'Hey, I can do this.' But finishing the 48 wasn't a goal of mine."

Unlike the bluebird day we got on the Franconia Ridge Loop in May, Mother Nature was not cooperating. As we strapped on our backpacks and began our ascent, it was obvious we had a long, wet hike ahead of us. We knew we would have scattered showers all day and there'd be no views from the summit.

"We had really adverse weather for the first time," said Hanson.

"We knew we were going to climb this giant mountain and see nothing. But, we're doing it anyway. As opposed to saying, 'It's cloudy out; we'll come back another day.'"

"The weather wasn't great," said Rice. "The weather is what you have to deal with, especially at elevation. It can also change. Yeah, we were going to be socked in on the summit, but so what."

We made our way up the Beaver Brook Trail and it didn't take long to hit the first of the cascades. The mist from the falls, combined with the day's precipitation, well, everything on trail was wet. This made the frequent wooden steps along the route especially slick. However, the beauty of the never-ending falls and the ongoing soundtrack they provided made the climb rewarding. We were also gaining elevation fast as the trail climbs nearly 2,000 feet in its first 1.5 miles.

"There's almost a mile of waterfalls along the lower half of the Beaver Brook Trail," said Rice. "That section is a steep-ass hike. It was gorgeous and kicking our butts at times. But the whole time I was thinking, 'Wow, that's really pretty.'"

At the 1.5-mile mark, and an elevation of 3,750, sits the Beaver Brook Shelter. We stopped there for a break and took off our packs. In addition to checking out the shelter, and its view to the northeast of the Franconia Range, we opted to have a beverage to celebrate knocking off two-thirds of the hike's elevation. While we still had 2.3 miles to the summit, we had only a bit more than 1,000 feet of elevation remaining to climb. During this time at the shelter, a group of backpackers showed up.

"I remember seeing them, three guys and two girls, and thinking they were way overloaded with gear," said Rice. "They were like super-rookies. The guys were way, way over-packed. But they were young enough, and in good enough shape, to handle it and it was awesome to see folks getting out. Good for them."

We left the shelter refreshed and a bit fueled up. There was an occasional shower, but never a steady rain. With the steepest part of the trail behind us, we made a big push for the summit. At 1.9 miles, the trail turns right and heads toward Mount Blue. There's a nice outlook during this stretch, just south of Mount Blue, with a great view into the Jobildunk Ravine. At 3.4 miles, the Beaver Brook Trail reaches the Benton Trail. A left turn and .4 miles south put us on the big, bald, mighty summit of Moosilauke.

"When we got up on the summit, it was pretty extreme weather up there," said Hanson. "We hunkered down in one of those bunkers; got out of the elements to eat and drink."

On top of Moosilauke are a series of circular rock shelters, designed for hikers to get out of the wind, and on this day, minimize the impact of the occasional hail and snow. They are also designed to contain hikers from leaving the trail to explore the open summit and endanger the alpine vegetation. Due to the weather and a thick cloud cover, just as expected, we really couldn't see anything from the summit. Yep, we were completely socked in.

"The summit was like a foreign land that day," said Rice. "We were up there and it was all brand new to us."

Stone bunkers on Moosilauke

We quickly got comfortable in one of the stone bunkers. We enjoyed the moment and passed around a flask of bourbon (Jim Beam). That helped warm us up a bit. There was a round of traditional snacks as we were sharing some beef jerky and trail mix, as well as crackers and cheese. Engler, always a bit of a nonconformist, had something a little different.

"I remember Engler with a can of Progresso soup," said Hanson, "and eating it cold."

"I often brought cans of food to eat while hiking," said Engler. "It was probably the saltiest one they had."

Eric Engler and trail food

Before we began our descent, we took a round of photos with the Moosilauke summit sign. These pictures in particular are a great reminder of the start of my NH 48 journey, especially when looking closely at the little details such as gear and clothing. On this hike, I'm wearing a knit hat that was given to me in the winter of 1992-1993 in Lake Placid, New York, while interning with the United States Luge Association. I figured that if it was good enough for Olympic athletes, well, I'd take it. I'm also wearing a pair of fleece San Jose Sharks gloves that I picked up free at a work event, the National Hockey League Retail Summit that summer. Of course, the lack of quality gear didn't matter that day.

"It was so awesome at the top. Just hanging out together," Engler told me. "You were really proud of it. You wanted an individual picture with the summit sign."

A close look at Rice in these photos shows he was carrying a tall, thick walking stick. It was something he often carried during these years while hiking.

"That's a two-pound stick. I could spin it around in my hand, and it was bent a few ways. It had a nice spot to hold on to for going up, and it had a nice spot that was great for going down," said Rice. "We almost burnt it once on an OA trip in Vermont, but Hanson said, 'You got a pretty nice hiking stick there, cut down by a beaver.' I was like, 'Yeah,' and I still have it to this day."

As we began our decent of the Beaver Brook Trail, Rice and Hanson slowly separated from Engler and me. It wasn't an issue and certainly wasn't a problem on the upper portion of the trail. They were just moving at a faster clip as Engler and I were being cautious due to the trail's wet condition. They would occasionally hold up and wait for us at various points including the Beaver Brook Shelter. However, this would be the last time we saw them until the parking lot. As a reminder, the shelter is 1.5 miles from the trailhead and some 2,000 feet above it. The route down, in the rain, was not to be taken lightly. When Engler and I reached the parking lot, I let Hanson and Rice know I was not happy with their decision to finish ahead of us. That in those conditions, we needed to stay together in case someone fell and got hurt. I couldn't carry Engler out by myself and, at 240 pounds, he certainly couldn't carry me. And I meant it.

"You scolded me and Rice at the bottom," said Hanson. "You were like, 'You guys should have waited for us.' But we got into a rhythm on the way down."

"I don't remember being scolded but I can imagine you doing that," Rice told me. "I do remember the gap between us. We had time for a beer when we got down waiting for you two. Hanson and I often have the same hiking pace. When we have met up for hikes together, we always do well and make good time."

Just as the Lafayette Place Campground parking lot was empty after the Kinsmans hike, the Beaver Brook Trailhead lot was essentially a ghost town as well. Our four cars were scattered about and as we dropped packs, removed boots, and began our goodbyes, there was a real sense of closure on the 2012 hiking season.

"Yeah, it was obvious that our hiking season was over," said Rice. "See you guys at the Gobble Gobble."

The Gobble Gobble is an annual horseshoe tournament held the day after Thanksgiving at my home in New Boston, NH. It was launched the year my wife and I bought our home (2001) and includes 10-14 Fitchburg State alumni spending a day outdoors. In the early years, it also included spouses and children. Hanson, Engler, and Rice are all regulars, which is also another piece of our bond. During the past 20-plus years, through all the job changes, moves, marriages, kids, mortgages, loss of parents, etc., we always spend a day—a great day—together during Thanksgiving weekend. Now, we were hiking partners.

"We took the hardest trail up Moosilauke," said Hanson. "And we did it in the rain, which the experts advise against. That series of waterfalls just goes on forever. Falls and falls and falls. It's really one of my favorite trails in the Whites. It's a magical hike."

"That was a great hike even though we were socked in and didn't have a view of anything that day," said Rice. "But we did it. We got our feet around the summit marker."

## CLIFF NOTES: WMS CHAPTER 4

 When hiking in groups, start together and finish together; separation on trail is fine but be sure to meet up at junctions.

 Bad weather doesn't mean a bad experience on trail.

 The hiking season doesn't ever really have to end.

**Facebook Post:**

Keith Gentili
October 22, 2012

MT. MOOSILAUKE (4,802)—Saw some snow, hail, and 50-60 mph winds en route to the summit of NH's 10th highest peak yesterday. But didn't see much from the top due to the clouds (nor did I have to see the Patriots fourth quarter). How about 10 points if you can identify the team logo on my gloves?

# 2013
# SOPHOMORE YEAR
# PEAKS #9–25

# CHAPTER 5
## Year 2, It's On

Date: Saturday, April 27, 2013
Mountain Range: Sandwich
Peak/Elevation (feet): Tecumseh 4,003*
Route (Out and Back): Mount Tecumseh Trail
Total Distance: 5 miles
Hiking Partners: Eric Hanson, Hannah Sparks
Road to 48: #9

Driving home alone on the evening of October 21, 2012, after summing Moosilauke, I knew my hiking season was over. It was a bittersweet moment as I had still yet to come down fully from the high of the Kinsmans climb. I finished 2012 with eight of the 48 mountains completed, which meant I was 17 percent of the way toward my goal. This also meant the pursuit of the NH 48 was now officially off and would be for the next six months. However, I would continue my studies all winter in preparation for the start of the spring hiking season.

The plan for 2013 would be to focus on mountains in the Sandwich Range, the seven southeastern-most peaks in the NH 48, as well as mountains located west of Route 302, specifically the Crawford Notch section between Twin Mountain and Bartlett. Targeting these summits would keep travel time to a minimum in Year 2. Plus, combining this with my original "one-hike-a-month approach," I was confident that I would make a run at the NH 48 halfway point by the end of the season.

As the calendar rolled into April, it was time to book the first hike of the new year. I chose Saturday, April 27 and the Osceolas. Team Hannahson—Eric Hanson and Hannah Sparks—signed on. The plan was to drive to the Mount Osceola trailhead on Tripoli Road, approaching from the Waterville Valley end. I met Team Hannahson just south of Concord at our friend (and fellow OAer) Ed

Murray's home. I left my car there and hopped into Hanson's 2011 Ford Taurus.

Things went smoothly all morning as we made our way north on I-93 and then northeast on Route 49 into the ski resort. As we began our drive west on the non-maintained Tripoli Road, it became apparent we had a challenge ahead of us. We were not that far past Livermore Road when the unplowed snow deepened and the road conditions worsened.

"We figured it's the spring, we'll be fine. But the snow just kept getting deeper as we were driving up Tripoli Road," said Hanson. "The Taurus had front-wheel drive and sat a bit low. I started to think I was going to beach us like a whale."

There were a couple moments when I thought, this is it, the journey is ending. We're not going to make it to the trailhead. Then, Hanson would work through a situation and we would push on. Okay, we're back. This is happening. But each success just led to another hill to climb and more snow to plow through. Hannah, who was riding shotgun, was beginning to feel uncomfortable. I, too, was also getting worried. Hanson powered on. Then, another hill. Hannah wisely turned around and said to me, "Don't you think it's time we turn around?"

"Yes, I do," I answered.

Hannah was the voice of reason amid a hiker-driven adventure that could have turned very bad, very fast. In our zest to get on trail and conquer the Osceolas, Hanson and I had lost sight of the present danger. We were in jeopardy of sliding off a road that was essentially unpassable, certainly for a vehicle without four-wheel or all-wheel drive.

"So I agreed to go back, by driving backwards on Tripoli Road in the snow—corn snow," said Hanson. "It made sense to just put it in reverse and go. We were fine. It never got to the point that we were stuck or even that close to it."

I do recall us sliding off what felt like the edge of the road as Hanson finally turned the car around, literally. But it didn't take too much effort to wiggle out of whatever mess we were in and get back into the center lane.

As we drove east on Tripoli Road, discussions turned to, well, now what? Hanson suggested we try the Greeley Pond Trailhead at Livermore Road. I pulled out the map. While it would certainly add mileage (about four miles total), the Greeley Pond Trail connects to the north end of the Mount Osceola Trail and we'd still get our two targeted summits, East Osceola and Osceola. Yes. We were back on and excited to get on trail.

We parked at the Livermore Road parking area, thrilled to be out of the car. It was still early in the day and the three of us were optimistic about the new plan. We laced up and set out on the Greeley Pond Trail. It was about four miles to the junction of the Mount Osceola Trail, where we would turn left (south). Another 1.3 miles straight on the Greeley Pond Trail puts hikers at the Kancamagus Highway (Route 112) trailhead.

We knew we had our work cut out but we were ready to chase it. Yet, it did not take long for us to notice the abundance of blowdowns and forest wreckage. The trail was a pure obstacle course. Time and time again, we had to navigate off trail, and circle back to re-join. We had to go over, under, and around fallen trees. There were a few water crossings that seemed like hike-enders, but we managed to push on. Then, we reached the Mad River crossing and saw the Knight's Bridge was washed out.

"I'll never forget the site of girders and bent steel I-beams," said Hanson. "And all the trees that were down. Tropical Storm Irene absolutely gutted the Whites and this area in particular."

Tropical Storm Irene hit New Hampshire on August 28, 2011. It dropped eight inches of rain into White Mountain rivers including the Mad and Pemigewasset. Reports indicated that debris such as fallen trees caused rivers to flood and re-route, wreaking havoc on surrounding areas. Thus, the Greeley Pond Trail, despite our best effort and intentions, was not going to get us to the Mount Osceola Trail. Not on this day, and, not until late in 2014 when it officially re-opened after major repairs.

"Whole sections of that trail got blown out. We made it as far as we could," said Hanson. "I remember seeing those bridge girders bent thinking, we aren't going further. So, we turned around."

For the second time that day, our plans changed. On the hike back to the Livermore Road parking area, we discussed one more option: Tecumseh. The trailhead was close and the hike to the top was just 2.5 miles. We felt we could summit before sunset and come down enjoying the end of the evening's Golden Hour. We even discussed hiking down the ski trail on the bottom section to enjoy the night sky. And just as we had pivoted earlier that morning along Tripoli Road, from the Mount Osceola Trail to the Greeley Pond Trail, we now set our sights on the Mount Tecumseh Trail.

"We were looking at the jaws of defeat," said Hanson. "But I knew Tecumseh was a legit option. It was a sunny and beautiful April day. We could still get a summit, a 48er."

MapQuest shows the drive from Livermore Road to Waterville Valley as 1.6 miles. It felt even shorter. We parked adjacent to the Mount Tecumseh Trailhead in the ski resort parking lot and got back on trail very quickly. We were on a mission. Hanson knew that Tecumseh, like Moosilauke, has a summit marker. We were going to get our boots around that marker. The three of us hit the trail at elevation 1,840 after 3pm and moved efficiently on the way up.

Just over a mile into the hike and about 700 feet of vertical gain, we reached a side path that leads to the edge of the ski trail. It's a nice spot to take in a view of the resort. We stopped briefly and noted it as an option on the way down, to return to the parking lot via the ski trail. We continued up the steepest section of the trail, and at 2.2 miles, we reached the junction of the Sosman Trail (elevation 3,840). A left on Sosman leads to the top of the ski area; we went right toward the summit and got our peak. In 2013, the Tecumseh summit was at 4,003 feet. Today, a new summit marker placed in 2019 has Tecumseh measuring 3,997 feet.

"We really did learn a little something from the Tecumseh hike," said Hanson. "We made a plan and thought we are going to do this, but then the mountains say, 'Oh no you're not,' because of the conditions. Tecumseh was a pure recover. A real plan B."

On the descent, we discovered boot skiing. The trail featured a soft, single track of snow that was melting. As darkness began to arrive, we made the call to trail run, then transition into a boot skiing position as much as Mother Nature would allow. We knew we were the last folks out on trail that night and it became another adventure

on a day that featured an interesting variety of adventures.

"It was wicked fun. I remember you texting me the next day that your knees were killing you," Hanson told me. "We were boot skiing huge swaths through the snow."

As we continued down, it became increasingly darker. Hanson was challenging me to resist using my headlamp. Rather, to let my eyes adjust to the conditions of the moment. He was so confident that the headlamp was unnecessary on this particular evening.

"You realize how dark it can be and you can still see," said Hanson. "Your eyes adjust. You can see in the darkness."

I played along for a while and was enjoying the game. It was working, sort of. We reached the side path to the ski trail and agreed to take this route back down to the parking lot. The view of the distant lights combined with the stars and night sky was just outstanding. Night hiking proved to be uniquely special and just as rewarding. Of course, every now and again I would catch my foot on something, stumble, and curse. This repeated itself a few times before Hannah said, "Just put your headlamp on before you really fall."

She was right. The voice of reason again.

*In 2019, a new summit marker was placed atop Mount Tecumseh with an elevation of 3,997 feet. Its status among the NH 48 continues to be a subject of debate within the hiking community.*

## CLIFF NOTES: WMS CHAPTER 5

🏃 Always be open to adjusting your trip as sometimes Mother Nature has a different plan for you.

🏃 Make your best effort to communicate clearly and efficiently at all times with your hiking partners.

🏃 Decisions on trail, or en route to the trail, need to involve all members of our group.

---

**Facebook Post:**

Keith Gentili
April 28, 2013

MT. TECUMSEH (4,003 ft.)—Although we ran into both road closures (snow on Tripoli Rd) and trail closures (Hurricane Irene damage) en route to the Osceolas, Plan B got us up Tecumseh, aka Waterville Valley, just before sunset Saturday night. That's Mt. Washington over my right shoulder in the distance.

# CHAPTER 6
# Executing the Plan

Date: Sunday, May 5, 2013
Mountain Range: Sandwich
Peak/Elevation (feet): East Osceola 4,156, Osceola 4,340
Route (Out and Back): Greeley Ponds to Mount Osceola
Total Distance: 7.6 miles
Hiking Partners: Eric Hanson, Keith Rice
Road to 48: #10, #11

Eight days. That's all it took to get back on trail in pursuit of the Osceolas after bagging Tecumseh. The plan had called for a spring summit of these two peaks, and I slotted them in for the following Sunday, May 5. Of course, with the wounds from the Tripoli Road failure still fresh, the trailhead target became the opposite end of the Greeley Pond Trail. Located along the Kancamagus Highway, the parking area is just a bit west of the infamous hairpin turn at the Hancock Overlook. Squeezing the Osceolas into early May was also part of a bigger hiking itinerary, which included a Bonds Traverse in just 11 days (May 16). "Sophomore Year" was underway. It was time to hike.

"I glommed onto this hike and I needed it. I felt like these were warm-up hikes, primer hikes, for the big trip we had planned to do—the Bonds and Zealand overnighter," said Rice. "I couldn't make the April hike of Tecumseh, and I didn't want to miss May. I made it a point to get the Osceolas."

Hanson was also on board as we agreed during the descent of Tecumseh that we needed to close the book on the Osceolas as soon as possible. The fact that we got out eight days later supports how hungry we were to not only stay on schedule, but to simply bag peaks. He also confirmed that he was, indeed, starting his NH 48 from the beginning. That the 20 or so summits he did during his Mount Rainier training would not be used toward his NH 48.

"This time, we came at the Osceolas from the other side," Hanson told me. "You were really reading the guides; you said 'It's going to be a steep hike.'"

"The parking lot was jammed," said Rice. "But we never saw that many folks on the trail. We couldn't figure out where they were hiking. It was weird."

Hanson, Rice, and I set out from the Greeley Pond Trailhead. It was a bright, sunny day. We traversed the first 1.3 miles quickly and reached the Mount Osceola Trail. At an elevation of 2,300 feet, this junction is a nice spot to prepare for the day's real work as the next 1.5 miles climbs 1,856 feet to the summit of East Osceola. But before pushing forward, we opted to hang out and have a cold beverage as our body temperatures had risen. We even explored the area a bit.

"Somebody saw a set of snowshoes behind a log near the trail junction. They were hidden, stashed somewhat," said Rice. "I thought, 'Why wouldn't you claim snowshoes you found in the middle of the woods.' But Hanson said, 'No. Somebody left them there on purpose because they didn't want to hike them up the mountain.' That's when I was introduced to the concept of ditching gear that wasn't needed. I really didn't know that was a thing."

The first .8 miles after the junction rises moderately. We churned it out to reach an elevation of 3,000 feet. From here, the peak of East Osceola is just .7 miles, but the next .5 miles represented the steepest section of the trail.

"Just after the junction, I remember it getting steep, steep, steep," said Rice. "That was an ass-kicking up to East Osceola. We knew that it would also be killer on the way down. It's just so steep."

The East Osceola summit is essentially viewless. With a little work, and additional hiking down side paths, there are lookouts to find. However, on this day, the goal was the next peak. Osceola. While we did take a moment to celebrate the summit, it wasn't long until we were moving again along the trail's snowy single track.

"May 5 is still early up there," said Hanson. "There was a lot of snow between the peaks; but it was a lot warmer than a week earlier."

"Getting over to Osceola wasn't bad," said Rice. "It was a monorail and we didn't have snowshoes or spikes yet. We were post-holing a bit. But I was in better shape than the previous year."

As we worked our way closer to Osceola, anticipation for the hike's upcoming signature feature, the Chimney, naturally began. I had read a lot about the Chimney, a vertical rock wall we would soon be facing and the difficulty many hikers had ascending it. I also knew it could be bypassed, but that never really seemed like an option for us. Hanson and Rice agreed. We were seeking the biggest challenge we could find and the Chimney was the one thing on this hike that really separated it from the other 48s. After all, plenty of the NH 48 routes are steep.

"Just before the Chimney, we ran into an older British couple," said Hanson. "They warned us about gnarly trail conditions on the Chimney. After the exchange, we sort of scoffed at them and the idea of not climbing it. We were starting to develop some bravado. We knew we were up for hiking in winter conditions. But it was pretty sketchy; I remember the ice and snow with kick holes."

We got up and over the Chimney safely and ripped out the final .5 miles to Osceola. A great big open rock summit, Osceola provides for big views and a real sense of accomplishment especially for hikers coming from the Kancamagus Highway as we did. Plus, there are old fire tower footings on the top. The fire tower was removed in 1985 by the Forest Service.

"I remember the climb kicking our ass because it was just so steep," said Rice. "But we crushed the day."

Hanson was on lunch duty for this hike and prepared the first hot summit meal of our NH 48 journey. He made macaroni and cheese, utilizing a fire tower footing as his kitchen surface. He had a small rocket stove and mess kit that worked nicely. Not surprisingly, Hanson also packed along some hot sauce to add a little kick to the mac-and-cheese. The sun was out, lunch was served, and the view of Mount Washington was crystal clear. It was another bluebird day in the Whites.

Hanson making lunch on one of the old fire tower foundations

"It was a good time on the summit. A lot of laughs that day. A real feel-good hike. But that is what the Whites are. You never know what you're going to get. That's why you have be in the moment. Even on the non-bluebird days, you can still have a helluva hike," said Rice. "There was a time we were on Mount Washington and we were hanging outside of the Lakes of the Clouds Hut with the hosts. We could see satellites floating across the sky. It was crystal clear and the hosts were saying, 'This is the best night of the summer. We haven't had a night this clear yet.' It just so happened we were there and got the best night of the summer."

The return trip from the Osceola summit was, not surprisingly, smooth. We were efficient in getting back over to East Osceola and careful descending the steepest part of the trail. When we reached the intersection of the Greeley Pond Trail, Rice checked on the pair of snowshoes that were stashed behind the log. They were gone. That made sense and felt right, as we trusted their rightful owner returned for them.

Also at this point, I was out of water, for real. The descent from East Osceola took some effort and I finished everything I had during that stretch. I was now thirsty and with 1.3 miles remaining to the parking lot, albeit flat, I wanted to hydrate. I was disappointed in myself for not carrying more water on the hike. I had the space in my pack (re: my behemoth 55-liter Gregory pack) but opted to go with just two liters.

"You were completely out of water and I filtered some out of the stream for you," Rice reminded me. "I filtered it through my charcoal pump and you were like 'This water is awesome; this water is better than my tap water.' You were genuinely impressed."

The water filter was only something I had read about in magazines at this point. I had no on-trail experience with them at all. So, I then quizzed Rice on all things water filter and he shared what he knew. I was sure that by the time we set out on the Bonds Traverse in 11 days, I would own a water filter. I was committed to never putting myself, or our group, in that situation again. I did the research online and bought the MSR MiniWorks EX Water Filter the following week. While it weighs a full pound, I still have it to this day and it remains a part of my backpacking trips. I also knew in that moment that Rice, like Hanson, was really a key part to the NH 48 journey.

"I liked going and wanted to be involved. I wanted to be on the hikes, but I still wasn't thinking about the 48," said Rice. "I had done a handful or so, but I wasn't interested in sending off for the patch at that point."

## CLIFF NOTES: WMS CHAPTER 6

🥾 Educate yourself on water filters. It is one item that may save your life.

🥾 If you see gear near a trail, don't assume it's lost or missing.

🥾 Hot lunch is always a good option, with a wide range of choices.

🥾 Be open to trail advice/feedback from others who have already traversed the route ahead of you.

**Facebook Post:**

Keith Gentili
May 7, 2013

MT. OSCEOLA (4,340 ft.)—Tripoli Rd. was still closed this weekend which meant hiking south from the Kanc. to get to the Osceolas. Lots of snow and tricky going but nice summit views.

# CHAPTER 7
# Hello Backpacking

Date: Thursday-Friday, May 16-17, 2013
Mountain Range: Twin
Peak/Elevation (feet): Zealand 4,260, West Bond 4,540,
Bond 4,698, Bondcliff 4,265
Route (Thru Hike): Zealand to Twinway to Bondcliff to
  Lincoln Woods
Total Distance: 20.6 miles
Hiking Partners: Eric Hanson, Eric Engler, Keith Rice
Road to 48: #12, #13, #14, #15

As May of 2013 rolled on, momentum was building for the first backpacking trip of the NH 48 experience. Hanson, Engler, and Rice were all committed. There was a two-week wave of emails, texts, and phone calls making arrangements, coordinating gear, and planning supplies. The trip was scheduled for the weekend before Memorial Day and, accordingly so, would be serving as Outdoor Adventure 18.

"We're not just backpacking," said Hanson. "We're backpacking over four 4,000-footers."

The plan was to launch from the Hancock Campground, which is just five miles east of Lincoln, along the Kancamagus Highway. Thanks to its first-come, first-served nature, we were confident a Thursday morning arrival in mid-May would result in securing campsites along the East Branch of the Pemigewasset River. We were right.

"We met at Hancock and combined all of our gear. We grabbed the best two sites at the campground," said Rice of walk-in sites 18 and 20. "We set up our tents and claimed our space. Then, we left three cars there and the four of us, with our packs, drove to Zealand."

Our Traverse of the Bonds would begin at the parking area at the southern terminus of Zealand Road. That is where the Zealand Trail (elevation 2,000) starts and that is where the four of us set out from for a two-day, 20-mile adventure. The first day's itinerary included visits to the Zealand Falls Hut, Zealand Falls, Zeacliff,

Zealand Mountain summit, Mount Guyot, and the Guyot Shelter, where we would spend the night. Day 2, we would hike the Bonds (West Bond, Mount Bond, and Bondcliff). After which, we would have a nine-mile hike out of the Pemigewasset Wilderness to the Lincoln Woods Visitor Center before crossing the Kancamagus Highway to return to the Hancock Campground, where our OA buddy Ed Murray would have a hot dinner waiting for us. It was a great plan.

"We had the right chemistry of guys. We were all there for the same purpose," said Rice. "It was better than going to church."

The 2.7 miles to Zealand Falls Hut went fast. We were running on adrenaline combined with a sense of purpose. Not even the beaver ponds, Zealand Pond, and some cool trail infrastructure (boardwalks) could slow us down as we motored right up to the hut's front steps. But from the moment we arrived, it was obvious we needed to slow down and hang out for a bit. There is just too much going on at Zealand (2,637 feet) to not spend some time absorbing it.

"Walking up to Zealand Falls Hut, that situation is so unique," said Rice. "The combination of the hut's porch and the falls being right there. It's just so phenomenal."

We made our way to the falls, found a spot with a view, and spread out. It had been a busy morning for the four of us and it was at this point, sitting amid Zealand Falls with water flowing around us, that we finally could relax. There was no more planning, no more gear to pack, no more driving or setting up tents. We were on our Traverse of the Bonds. It was happening.

"I think how blessed we were to be there," said Engler. "It's kind of the overall feeling I get when I see the pictures from this trip. I am not a big fan of some of the hikes, any over 12 miles, but when you get up there, you feel blessed to be there."

Just 1.3 miles from the hut along the Twinway sits Zeacliff (3,600 feet), a stunning location with a nearly unmatchable view of the Pemigewasset Wilderness and, specifically, Mount Carrigain. It's impossible to sit atop Zeacliff and not feel something for the Whites.

"I understand Hanson's claim," said Rice. "To bring yourself to a place where its enormity helps put things into perspective."

Following the Twinway, we had 1.6 miles to the summit of Zealand Mountain (4,260 feet). Zeacliff Pond is along this stretch and delivers another stunning view and reminder of the uniqueness of the White Mountains' ponds. While Zealand marked the trip's first 4,000-footer, its viewless summit has only a wooden sign hanging in a tree to celebrate. Nonetheless, we were firing on all cylinders at this point and getting excited about the next peak, Mount Guyot (pronounced Gee-oh).

"The hike up to the Guyot summit was special," said Rice. "It's just such a killer spot."

At 4,580 feet, Mount Guyot is a signature peak in this area of the Whites. It has a huge double summit and provides outstanding views of both the Franconia Range and Pemigewasset Wilderness. However, Guyot is not considered a 4,000-footer by the AMC because its summit is less than 200 feet above the col—the lowest point of a ridge between two peaks—separating it and South Twin Mountain (4,902 feet).

"Guyot is my favorite peak in the Whites that I climbed during my 48," said Hanson.

We dropped our packs on the summit of Guyot and got comfortable fast. We had hiked seven miles to this point and only had a mile, downhill, left to the Guyot Shelter. It was time to have some eats, and drinks, and enjoy the view, especially that of the Bonds. We would be hiking them the next day and there they were, sprawled out in front of us. Rugged and huge, with no sign of mankind.

"It was so beautiful out there on Guyot," said Engler.

We really enjoyed our time on the summit. In part because we were now fully immersed in the journey. Guyot was not a destination, just a spot we stopped along the way that will always be remembered because of this day. The four of us had not only settled into a groove together, but we each had found our own place, our own stride. It was evident that the trust and support that began to take shape on the Moosilauke hike was beginning to evolve and mature. The Allman Brothers Band called it "hitting the note," when everything came together exactly right. The Fitchburg State Hiking Club was hitting the note on the summit of Guyot.

"Between the weather and the time spent on the Guyot summit," said Hanson, "the Day 1 hike was special."

And it wasn't over yet. We made our way down Guyot and the Twinway, turning left on the Bondcliff Trail. It's .8 miles down to the side trail to the Guyot Shelter and, along the way, hikers get one of the unparalleled views of the Franconia Ridge. Looking west, in the forefront sits Owl's Head, and behind it, the high peaks of Lafayette and Lincoln. It's one of my favorite Golden Hour spots in the Whites. When we finally arrived at the shelter, we found it as well as all of the tent platforms, vacant.

"We had the shelter to ourselves," said Hanson. "And we saw nobody anywhere."

"I was exhausted when I got there," said Engler of the Guyot Shelter. "I remember you still had your lanyard on, with the map, in the shelter."

It's true, and that lanyard can be seen in many of the trip's photos. I was obsessed with trail maps during this time. I always had to know where we were, as well as what was ahead of us and what was behind us. Thus, I stored my Exploring New Hampshire's White Mountains Waterproof TOPO Map & Guide in a ticket lanyard and wore it around my neck on many hikes while an "underclassman." This meant I didn't have to stop and remove my pack to get my bearings. It worked. Of course, we were now at the shelter and I finally took it off. It was time to have fun, to rip it up.

"We did really well at the Guyot Shelter. We got silly and stupid. We were sort of renegades that night. Not everybody overnight hikes with beer and booze," said Rice. "A lot of the healthy folks that are backpacking are in bed at dusk and up at dawn. And that's cool. To each their own. Hike your own hike. But the time at Guyot Shelter that night was a real highlight."

The fact that we were alone helped fuel our fire. After a variety of appetizers (trail mix, cheese and crackers, shrimp), we cooked up a series of Mountain House Chili Mac sacks and as each one got emptied, the chorus to the 1966 Martha Reeves & The Vandellas song "Jimmy Mack" would appear. *"Oh Chili Mac, when are you coming back?"* In between, a wave of vodka-lemonades and hard Arnold Palmers were poured and served as our makeshift, Nalgene-bottled bar came together nicely. We packed in a bunch of the Crystal Light packets and we were using them. Between the dehydrated meals and endless mixed drinks, we were ripping through liters and liters of water. Not a problem.

"The spring is right next to the shelter. It's just awesome," said Rice. "Some shelters you have to walk 100 yards or further. But they built the Guyot Shelter right on top of the spring. Every shelter should have that."

It was a fun night of celebration that would eventually wind down. Engler and Rice took on the responsibility of hanging our food out of the reach of bears. Hanson, who is notoriously fast to fall asleep, climbed into his sleeping bag. I was excited to do the same and debut another new gear purchase, the Kelty Cosmic Down 20 Sleeping Bag. I did my research and got it for about $140 delivered. Weighing just over two pounds and filled (to 550) with duck down, it's both light and warm.

"We went to hang the bear bag over near the outhouse. We hear you bitching about something in the shelter. You were loud," Engler told me. "We were thinking 'What is he doing?' And it went on for a while. We kept trying to figure out what you were doing."

I had bought that sleeping bag brand new and just could not get the zipper to work. I was totally confused in the moment and not happy. Did I not test it when I first got it? Did the zipper come broken or did I just break it, right now in this shelter on the very trip I bought it for? Could this really be happening?

"When Engler and I went to hang the bear bag at Guyot, you were going off on your new sleeping bag," said Rice. "We found out later the zipper was broken. But we didn't know that at the time and you were losing your mind. We never even thought of a gear problem. We were wondering if Hanson went down; fell off the shelter deck. Maybe he's crumpled in the rocks. We get back and Hanson's snoring up a storm and we ask you what's wrong and you say your sleeping bag zipper is broken."

In the end, I had damaged the zipper. It was my fault. Too many drinks likely led me to being rough with my gear. It's not surprising and not the first, or last, time something like that happened. Yep, silly and stupid.

"I remember you were so disappointed with the bag," said Engler. "But it was user error."

That error essentially turned my Kelty Cosmic 20 into a quilt for about five years. I did finally find a seamstress to fix the zipper properly. My wife uses that bag regularly to this day and it still delivers a great night's sleep. As for that moment, the good news was Hanson didn't fall off the shelter's deck. The bad news was he was snoring loudly.

"Because all you guys snore so much, I slept outside, maybe 50 feet away from the shelter," said Engler. "I found a mossy area and threw my bag down, but it rained. My bag was wet when I woke up."

The morning brought a few rounds of coffee with Baileys and Pop-Tarts. It's my go-to hiking breakfast and never fails. Easy to make, easy to consume, easy to clean up. And very tasty. We got packed up pretty quickly and departed the Guyot Shelter headed for West Bond, which was only .7 miles away.

"West Bond was easy to get to," said Rice. "We slack-packed it up the spur trail, but the summit was socked in."

West Bond is known for providing visitors with one of the best views in the Whites. For some gridders, those who hike the NH 48 in all 12 months (576 total summits) over a period of time, West Bond is a favorite peak. On this day, we had no idea what view we were missing. But as we made our way toward Bond, the sky began to clear. It's a half-mile back down the West Bond spur trail, then another half-mile up the Bondcliff Trail to the Bond summit. By the time we reached the peak, the weather was nearly ideal.

"It's just a whole other level," said Hanson of the Bonds. "It's like being in the West. There's nothing made by man out there. Just a sliver of the trail."

The 1.2 miles between Bond and Bondcliff is arguably as beautiful as any stretch in the Whites. It puts hikers on pure sensory

overload. The combination of forest, mountains, and sky here is an ideal setting for folks to find that "hiker high." It's an unmistakable feeling of being present, of being in the moment, and being happy. Bondcliff has that power.

"It was totally epic. Unparalleled," said Hanson. "I remember being on the ridge, crossing the Bonds and thinking, this is a Top 10 hike of all time for me. And it always will be."

"I wouldn't argue with that," said Rice. "It was one of my favorite hikes."

When we reached Bondcliff, our final peak of the trip, we took some time to hang out on the cliff. We got a few signature photos and I have one of them printed on canvas, hanging in my home office. It's a reminder of that first backpacking trip of the NH 48.

"That hike was two days, 20 miles. Just awesome," said Rice. "When we were on Bondcliff, we were thinking how cool it was. But that is a serious spot. That's death to the west if you go off. You can't Rambo that. It's why those pictures we got on Bondcliff are so great."

After Bondcliff, we had nine miles to return to the Kancamagus Highway and Hancock Campground.

"All we had left was the trek down the Bondcliff Trail to the Lincoln Woods Trail," said Rice. "Then we hiked the rest of the way out and it was great, just as we planned it. Ed was at the campsite

Bondcliff

waiting for us."

The Traverse of the Bonds really did go just as we planned it. Like Hanson and Rice, it is certainly one of my favorite hikes of all time. Not only did it deliver everything I hoped, but it also fueled the NH 48 journey for all of us and accelerated our education. However, for Engler, it wasn't necessarily the perfect hike.

"I only went on a couple overnight hikes after that. Hiking with all that extra gear was just too much. I was exhausted after that hike. I learned that I had zero longevity," he said. "At that time, I couldn't have done it by myself. That was the interesting thing about it for me. There was a feeling of a safety net having the four of us there, knowing one of us would have the thing we needed. And it's so pretty when you look back on the photos."

## CLIFF NOTES: WMS CHAPTER 7

 If your group is not alone at a shelter, be respectful of others and their desire to hike their own hike, be it an early dawn start or a leisurely noon sojourn.

 Make time for the unique features found along each hike such as waterfalls, lookouts, and ponds.

 On overnight backpacking trips, bring more than just essentials... but be careful to track your pack's overall total weight.

 Take your pack out, full, for a test drive before departing on your trip.

### Facebook Post:

Keith Gentili
May 20, 2013

TRAVERSE OF THE BONDS—Made the 20-mile trek from Zealand to Lincoln Woods Thursday and Friday. Day 1 stops featured: Zealand Falls, Zeacliff, Zealand Mt., Mt. Guyot, and the Guyot Shelter. Day 2 included West Bond, Mt. Bond, and Bondcliff. Saw some snow, hail, rain, and high winds.

# CHAPTER 8
# Embracing the Brutality

Date: Saturday, June 22, 2013
Mountain Range: Sandwich
Peak/Elevation (feet): North Tripyramid 4,180, Middle
   Tripyramid 4,140
Route (Lollipop): Livermore to Mount Tripyramid to Livermore
Total Distance: 11.1 miles
Hiking Partner: Eric Hanson
Road to 48: #16, #17

Riding the momentum of the Bonds hike, I was eager to get something planned for June and it needed to be part of the Sandwich Range. I wanted to be sure to complete that region during the 2013 hiking season. My confidence and conditioning were high at this time. In between hikes, I was running regularly and had gotten my weight down to 238; the lowest of my adult years. On non-hiking weekends that summer, I was pushing myself in hopes of running a half marathon in the fall.

The previous fall, I ran the Squantum 5 in Quincy, Massachusetts, and got a taste of the competitive side of road racing. This scenic five-mile course featured ocean views, a nice climb, and a field of real runners. Plus, the post-race party was on a pier, sponsored by Harpoon, and the band included a few of my Fitchburg State buddies. In short, it was much more than a community 5K, which I had come to really enjoy running but was all I really knew at the time.

While I finished Squantum cleanly and was proud of my time (53:40), I was not only at the back of the pack, I was the final finisher who never walked at some point on the course. How do I know that? A motorcycle cop was waiting for me at each mile mark. As I neared him, he would call it in to race organizers on his radio. "The big guy in the orange shirt just reached mile 3." I really got a kick out of it. I was the true Clydesdale that day surrounded by hundreds of thoroughbreds. During the summer of 2013, I would attempt long runs of six-plus miles, sometimes completing up to eight miles or more in hopes of improving my overall pace and conditioning.

Thus, taking on the Tripyramids now, which would be a real test, made sense. As part of the ongoing NH 48 curriculum, the trip had to be via the toughest route. That meant a long hike (11.1 miles), ascending the North Slide, and descending the South Slide. It's worth noting that both of these sections of trail are part of the "The Terrifying 25," a White Mountains list created by hiker/author Trish Herr and her daughters Alex and Sage. The list celebrates interesting trails that "have slides, rock scrambles, and boulder caves."

As was the norm during these first two years, Hanson was on board. We met just southwest of Concord, at the Park & Ride off I-89 at exit 2, and traveled together from there. Not surprisingly, he was late. Hanson was often late but, surprisingly, it never bothered me. In fact, waiting for Hanson became a part of many hikes that I enjoyed. It gave me more time to prepare, whether it was packing, stretching, reading maps, or studying the guides. Sometimes I would just clean and organize my car as it always had a lot of extra gear. To me, it was all part of the overall NH 48 adventure and I loved it.

The drive to the trailhead included a return to the Waterville Valley area and Tripoli Road. We parked at the same spot, the Livermore Road parking area (elevation 1,580 feet), as we did for our failed attempt at the Osceolas. However, this time we set out on the Livermore Trail as opposed to the Greeley Pond Trail. We had 2.6 miles ahead of us to the point where the Mount Tripyramid Trail comes in from the South Slide. Another mile and the trail turns right at an elevation of 2,400 feet toward the North Slide. From here, it was 1.2 miles to the summit with 1,780 feet of vertical gain. It was sunny and warm and we were ready to climb.

"I was really impressed with the North Slide," said Hanson. "I had seen it before but had not climbed it. It was a real challenge going up it, and it was very humid that day."

We made our way up the slide methodically, often knocking off small sections and stopping to take in the view behind us. It was obvious in the moment; we were going straight up and we were relishing it. We were using our hands regularly and watching our feet very closely. There were loose rocks and big rocks, as well as slabs of granite at times. The North Slide delivered everything we were seeking. It was a big adventure and it was a test. There were moments we had to be extremely careful while, at other times, we moved swiftly enjoying our relative climbing prowess. We reached the summit of North Tripyramid at 4,180 feet, glazed in a heavy sweat, hungry, and thirsty.

The North Slide

"I remember you serving me a hot lunch while we were getting killed by black flies," Hanson told me. "We had to cover everything up."

I was on lunch duty this time and, after Hanson's macaroni-and-cheese effort on Osceola, I wanted to cook up something with sustenance. My wife had recently made mostaccioli, a lazy-lasagna-like dish featuring pasta, peppers, onions, and a meat sauce, and I was packing a Ziploc sack of leftovers. I fired up my backpacking stove and we were soon in business. However, the black flies were already eating. It was June 22 in the Whites, and it was humid with a chance of rain. Ideal conditions for black flies. We quickly went to a "no-skin exposed" strategy and that helped. We got comfortable with cold drinks and a hot lunch was being served.

"During that lunch, you told me about your brother and his legal woes and the axe. I'll never forget that," said Hanson. "You told me the whole story, how he essentially threatened his boss with his axe. It was very shocking to me. I'm used to hearing sad stories about divorce or someone being fired; not axe stories. Someone like you having a brother who would wield an axe, I remember hoping it would turn out for the best."

My brother Steven did essentially threaten his boss while "carrying" an axe. Twice his boss's dog had bitten him, and he was not satisfied with the way things were being handled. My brother, a lumberjack and woodsman in northern Maine, made the very bad decision, before entering his boss's home to discuss the matter, to grab something from his truck, his axe. If he had been a golfer, perhaps he would have grabbed a golf club. I don't know. But it didn't end well and my brother's legal problems, which started that day, haunted him for the rest of his life.

As we wrapped up lunch, it started to rain lightly. We trekked across the ridge quickly on the Mount Tripyramid Trail. Our next 4,000-footer, Middle Tripyramid (4,140), represented the halfway point of the day's hike as we were now 5.6 miles from the trailhead. While we were still experiencing scattered showers, we celebrated the summit, and enjoyed the nearby view to the west of Waterville Valley and beyond. As we worked toward South Peak, the rain became a bit steadier. And with the steep descent of the South Slide ahead of us, the conditions were becoming a concern. Our memory of the Flume Slide hiker who had fallen a year earlier in wet conditions had not faded yet.

The South Slide

Hanson and I were careful climbing down, repeating the mantra, "Nobody falls up a mountain." This helped us, and we got down the slide slowly and safely. Plus, the views on the way down from the South Peak are so great that it lessens the squeeze. Yet, we still had more than four miles to return to the trailhead.

"As it was pouring on us on the way back, I kept thinking we should be back at the car by now but they moved the lot," said Hanson. "I hated that they moved the parking lot back. So the walk from the trailhead to the Mount Tripyramid Trail became so much further."

We eventually reached the car. The 11.1 miles resulted in a full day/eight hours on trail. The first leg gave us a real lesson in vertical gain thanks to the steepness of the North Slide. The animal kingdom challenged us on the second leg as the black flies feasted on us before we covered up all of our exposed skin. And on the third leg, it was Mother Nature who opened up the skies, and let the rain test our footing on the descent of the South Slide and return to the car. We passed that test. It was a great day and we embraced all that came our way. It was another part of our ongoing education.

"We got rained on so bad, and were so wet, that we stopped at a gas station in Campton before getting on the highway," said Hanson. "I bought a touristy Live Free or Die T-shirt to drive home in. I was just so soaked. And I wore that T-shirt until it wore out."

## CLIFF NOTES: WMS CHAPTER 8

🚶 Always check and track the weather before hiking, including the higher-elevation conditions.

🚶 Wind, mud, and bugs can affect a hike as much as rain, snow, and temperatures.

🚶 Always keep drive-home clothes, as well as your favorite beverages (hot or cold), in the car for the post-hike wind down.

**Facebook Post:**

Keith Gentili
June 23, 2013

View from the top of the Tripyramids North Slide Saturday; rain held off until we hit the summit and made for a wet but nice and cool trip down the South Slide back to Waterville Valley. Total trip: 11 miles, 3,000 feet in elevation, 8 hours. The North Slide Trail up to North Tripyramid climbs 1,700 feet in just 1.2 miles; that's straight up at times. For the record, these rocks slid down in 1885. Two more 4,000-footers off the NH 48er list—17 down and 31 to go.

# CHAPTER 9
## Going Solo

Date: Wednesday, July 31, 2013
Mountain Range: Sandwich
Peak/Elevation (feet): Whiteface 4,020, Passaconaway 4,043
Route (Loop): Blueberry Ledge to Rollins to Dicey's Mill
Total Distance: 12 miles
Hiking Partners: None
Road to 48: #18, #19

For the first time since launching the NH 48 plan, it was difficult to schedule the month's hike. I knew it was going to be Mount Whiteface and Mount Passaconaway as that would complete the peaks of the Sandwich Range, one of my goals for 2013. But my hiking partners were just not available, and that was understandable. Life's combination of work, family, and summer vacations took priority, and rightfully so.

As July was ending, I knew I couldn't fall short of my personal goal of hiking once per month. To keep the streak alive, I took a vacation day from work on the last day I could—Wednesday, July 31. This meant I would be hiking solo, and that would be a first for my NH 48 journey. I was excited, as I knew this day had to come at some point. I realized to finish the 48 by my 48th birthday, I would have to get out when I could regardless of everyone else's schedule. My wife Carrie was not as thrilled.

"It concerned me. I did not like you hiking alone," said Carrie. "I was worried that you might have a medical emergency, not necessarily a heart attack, just some unexpected occurrence on the trail—an accident. But I was never concerned about you getting lost or being unprepared. You always did your research. You were meticulous in mapping out your hike and leaving me the details. I didn't always check them, but I knew they were on the refrigerator."

Part of my NH 48 approach did include being a good communicator with my family. I needed their support and understanding to make the NH 48 happen. It was a long play. I had to be good. Thus, I always left my hike's details where everyone could see them. Sometimes my daughters would get interested and ask me about the trails and where I was headed. I'd show them the map and tell them the highlights, what makes a certain hike unique such as a waterfall or summit view or unique rock formation. Of course, sometimes I would say that the hike was very dangerous and if daddy didn't make it home, you know he loves you. Ha.

As for the notes I left on the refrigerator, I would list the mountain, the planned route, how many miles it was, and the expected time on trail. For example, the note for this trip would have said something like this:

*Whiteface Passaconaway Loop*

*Up Blueberry, Down Dicey's Mill - 12 Miles*

*On Trail 11am to 8pm*

"I always liked that you would tell me how long each hike would take and when I could expect to hear from you," said Carrie. "You always texted me when you got back to the car and when you thought you'd be home. You often sent summit photos, so I knew you made it up the mountain. Part of the reason I was always nervous when you were hiking solo was because of the time you fell hiking in West Virginia and lost your watch."

In September of 1997, I was living in a small farmhouse in Glen Allen, Virginia, on a nice sprawling piece of property. One of my roommates was a Virginia Tech alum named Bill Ellis, who went by "Hokie Bill." A lifelong Virginia Tech season-ticket holder, Bill loves Hokie football as much as he loves a "bowl with" from the Texas Tavern in his hometown of Roanoke, Virginia. That's Star City jargon for a bowl of chili with onions. Bill offered me a ticket to see his nationally ranked Hokies host the Syracuse Orangemen on September 13, 1997, in Blacksburg, Virginia. I jumped on it. But I also jumped at the opportunity to do some hiking in the southwest corner of the state as that was foreign land to me. After some digging around online, I set my sights on Bluestone State Park in Hinton, West Virginia. Less than an hour and half from Virginia Tech's Lane Stadium, it was perfect. I'd travel from Richmond Friday after work and camp Friday night. Then, hike Saturday morning and into the early afternoon, before heading to Blacksburg for a little tailgating and 6pm kickoff.

Everything went according to plan until I fell. I was having a nice day on trail, but I opted to bushwhack back to my car—a shortcut that would get me some extra time tailgating Hokie style (i.e., bourbon and bbq). Bad call. I quickly found myself on a surprisingly steep slope that didn't end until it dropped right off and met a state park road. As I worked my way down, I began relying more and more on the assistance of small trees and any of the sparse hand holds I could reach. Soon, I was in a real jam.

Then, I made a second bad decision. I took a step I didn't want to take. I should have retraced my route and went back up, but I didn't. I was much younger and inexperienced as a hiker. I took the step and my foot never landed. I went right into a tumble, rolled multiple times, and free fell about six feet. *Thud.* Luckily, I hit nothing along the way and landed clean. I was not injured. Sore? Yes.

After I got my bearings, I went to check the time but my watch was missing. Damn. Carrie had given me that watch the previous November in celebration of the five-year anniversary of our first kiss (November 23, 1991). We went to Niagara Falls, the Canadian side, and she gave it to me during dinner overlooking the falls. It was special. I decided to go back up and look for it. Another bad idea. It wasn't long before I realized it was just too steep. I turned around and cut my losses.

I did get myself to Blacksburg later that afternoon. Bill, along with his parents and Hokie family, were great hosts. I learned the real difference between pulled pork and shredded pork that day. At one point, Bill did ask me if I was okay as he felt I was a bit reserved during the tailgate. I told him about my fall and assured him that I was fine. As for the game, Bill's mom snuck bourbon into Lane Stadium in a Ziploc bag and the No. 22 Hokies rolled 31-3. Great day.

A strange thing did happen on my three-hour drive home that night from Blacksburg to Richmond. I ran out of gas between Waynesboro and Charlottesville, Virginia. I was driving east on I-64 and just never checked my gas gauge. Not once. This was before cars had low-gas dashboard lights and provided your "Distance to Empty." I managed to get to an off-ramp and was fortunate to catch a ride a mile or so to a gas station and back. Call it southern hospitality. Based on the mileage I have put on cars that I have owned since graduating from Fitchburg State in 1993, I believe I have driven a million miles. This is the only time I ever ran out of gas.

"You probably had a concussion," said Carrie. "That hike has always stayed with me and every time you went hiking solo, the memory would, at some point, go through my mind."

Another thing that was unique about the Whiteface-Passaconaway Loop was the drive to the trailhead. This would be the first of the NH 48 adventures that didn't include a visit to Franconia Notch or time along the Kancamagus Highway or Tripoli Road. I loved that. Rather, the drive to the Ferncroft Road trailhead in Wonalancet featured a scenic ride through parts of New Hampshire's Lakes Region and the towns of Ashland, Holderness, and Sandwich. It meant driving along the north shore of Squam Lake, where the Oscar-winning film *On Golden Pond* was filmed. And it meant a drive past the Wonalancet Union Church. Situated at the north end of a hay field with the mountains as a backdrop, it's an idyllic, stop-you-in-your-tracks New England postcard of a church. When you see that church, you know you'll soon be on trail.

I parked at Ferncroft (elevation 1,140 feet) and laced up anxiously. I had everything I needed and just wanted to get moving. I knew this was a big hike in terms of mileage and, while I was looking forward to descending during the evening's Golden Hour, I didn't necessarily want to be night hiking solo. Leaving the parking lot, I started walking up Ferncroft Road, also a first for the NH 48. And also cool. It's a neat feeling, making your way to somewhere big by foot, passing New Hampshire camps and homes wondering what might be happening inside, and if anyone is watching you pass by. It's one of the real secrets of the NH 48 puzzle, just how different so many of the hikes are and how they take you to such varying places in the state. Only after the puzzle is completed does the whole picture come into view.

I soon hopped on the cutoff toward the Blueberry Ledge Trail. The cutoff is only .2 miles shorter, but the real win is that it extends your walk along the Wonalancet River. Once back on the Blueberry Ledge Trail, about two miles from the parking lot and at 2,150 feet, the real climbing begins. There's an outlook around 3,000 feet, after which the trail starts to ascend steadily. The final half-mile includes some legit rock scrambling and great views. There's an open ledge looking toward the Lakes Region at 3,600 feet that provides a view that is quintessential New Hampshire and it does not feature the White Mountains—another unique aspect of this hike. I stopped here for a while to take pictures, fuel up on water, and have a granola bar.

From here, the steepest section of rock awaits. It caught me by surprise but had a nice reward at the top: an exceptional view looking east at the unmistakable summit of Mount Chocorua. Whiteface's summit (4,020 feet) is just up the trail and it was my targeted destination lunch spot. I changed shirts and got comfortable. I had the place to myself and wasn't in a rush to start the 2.3-mile hike across the top of "The Bowl" to Passaconaway. The Bowl is a glacial cirque that features a virgin forest (never been logged), as well as 1,500 acres tagged Research Natural Area, or RNA.

The Bowl

Eventually, I made my way toward Passaconaway along the Rollins Trail. There are a couple of lookouts on that route that provide a nice view of The Bowl below. Rollins meets the Dicey's Mill Trail about a mile from the summit at 3,300 feet. The final ascent to Passaconaway's summit climbs 700 feet to 4,043 and requires a good push. Early evening was starting to arrive as I hit the peak. I got a nice photo looking west of the twilight shining on me and the Sandwich Range Wilderness. It was a nice moment. I had hiked 7.5 miles so far, and had 4.5 miles remaining to return to the trailhead. I was looking forward to going down.

Because I had read so much about this hike, I knew I'd be finishing up with a walk through a residential property. That I would literally complete this 12-mile loop by passing a farmhouse, heading straight down a driveway, and walking back onto Ferncroft Road. What I didn't realize is that I'd catch it just as sunset was ending and the night was starting to pop. As I stepped off the Dicey's Mill Trail and stepped into the back field of the farm, the sky was aglow in both colors and stars. I got chills while traversing the property and thought how wonderful it was that the owners not only allowed hikers but seemingly encouraged them. I was "hitting the note" on trail again, and that adrenaline carried me right down Ferncroft Road to my car, the only one remaining in the lot.

I removed my pack, boots, and socks. I slipped on my soft-cotton driving T-shirt and flip-flops. But I couldn't leave. The parking area abuts an open field filled with wild flowers. The sky was just too beautiful to say goodbye to. It was night but it wasn't dark. I sat in the lot, texted my wife, and slowly drank the only beer that was waiting in the cooler in my car. Sometimes when folks ask me why I hike, I think of those 30 minutes or so I sat alone in the Ferncroft Road parking lot and smile.

🥾 Always leave your hiking itinerary in the same spot for your family/friends/roommates and be as detailed as possible, including noting the expected times on trail.

🥾 When hiking alone, check in from the summit and/or provide updates of your progress.

🥾 Don't be in a rush to leave the trailhead parking lot upon returning to your car.

**Facebook Post:**

Keith Gentili
August 10, 2013

WHITEFACE-PASSACONAWAY LOOP—I got one hike in last month with two summits: Whiteface (4,020) and Passaconaway (4,043). Nice loop of 12 miles and 3,800 feet total climb. That's 19 of 48 down. Here's some photos of the Lakes Region and Mount Chocorua from Whiteface. The sunset shot is facing west on Passaconaway. Yep, came down in the dark via headlamp.

# CHAPTER 10
## Crushing It

Date: Friday, August 23, 2013
Mountain Range: Presidential
Peak/Elevation (feet): Jefferson 5,716
Route (Lollipop): Caps Ridge to The Link to Castle to Caps Ridge
Total Distance: 6.7 miles
Hiking Partner: Eric Hanson
Road to 48: #20

Just as planning the July hike was a challenge, finding a date in August that worked for others was not happening. I threw out a couple of suggestions but nothing materialized. It was frustrating as I had the hiker's itch to get on trail. But as much as I thrived and embraced hiking solo the previous month, I also missed my hiking partners. As the calendar reached the back half of the month, my family vacation was coming into play. So much so, that it became apparent the best chance I had of keeping the once-a-month streak alive was to build a 4,000-footer into the Gentili family camping trip.

Carrie and I had booked five days and nights at the Mountain Lake Camping Resort in Lancaster, NH. We were traditionally state park campers, but a key piece to this trip was a two-day visit to Santa's Village in Jefferson, NH. During their childhood, we would take our daughters to Story Land one year, Santa's Village the next. Eventually, as a family, we outgrew Story Land but we still try to schedule an annual trip to Santa's Village during the Christmas season. There's something special about that place that really brings a family together. I have eight souvenir-photo snow globes to prove it as, with age, the four of us fill up more and more of a Skyway Sleigh (these days we split into pairs on this ride).

Just a 15-minute drive from Santa's Village, the Mountain Lake resort offered all the activities to make a family camping trip complete: canoeing, fishing, biking, and a swimming pool. In the summer of 2013, our daughters were 11 (Julia) and 9 (Sarah) and really enjoyed all of these things, to a point, as well as the usual camping traditions such as cooking on a fire, making s'mores, and sleeping in a tent. On that trip in particular, Sarah caught a nice-sized largemouth bass from our canoe while Julia was hooked on fishing from the lake's dock because she could watch the little fish nibble on her bait. I had put the bug in my wife's ear earlier in the week that I might disappear Friday morning to go hiking. While she didn't love the idea, she certainly understood what it meant to me.

"It's that fine line of wanting to keep the family unit together, doing things together, while understanding each member has to have their own interests and pursuits. I certainly support that," said Carrie. "You were doing something on your own and it did not involve me and the kids. But I was supportive because I knew it was something you wanted to do, and I was also proud. I knew it was important to you and you were challenging yourself to do it."

The plan involved Mount Jefferson and the Caps Ridge Trail, which was just 20 miles away from the campground. At an elevation of 3,008 feet, the Caps Ridge Trailhead is the highest-elevation trailhead on a public road in the White Mountains. This meant less vertical gain and climbing, which equals less time on trail. Plus, the summit of Jefferson is only 2.5 miles from the parking lot. So, unlike the 12 miles of the Whiteface-Passaconaway loop or 11 miles of the Tripyramids and Kinsmans hikes, I was only going for a five-mile trek. This all added up to my convincing the Mrs. I would be back in time for a late lunch. How could she say no?

"It was never about the distance of the hike but the window of time that you would be gone, meaning from the time you left until the time you got back," said Carrie. "I did like that the kids were seeing you pursue the 48, setting a goal, and understanding that it was a healthy thing. It was good for them."

But then I got another idea. It didn't exactly match my presentation to Carrie, but it wasn't exactly a change of plans.

"There was this day you were camping with your family," said Hanson. "And you texted me, 'We gotta do Jefferson.'"

I couldn't help myself. I missed my hiking partners and I knew Hanson also had the itch to get back on trail. So, I thought I'd try. And because it was a Friday as opposed to a weekend day, I felt there might be a chance he would sign on. But I also knew he was juggling a few things. He was working on building a life together with Hannah. In fact, Team Hannahson had a lot of big things going on at that time.

"Hannah was pregnant with Elsa and she was still working," said Hanson, whose daughter was born in March of 2014. "And I closed on our house August 1. But before we could move in, I ripped out the carpets and started painting. I didn't want Hannah inhaling all the crap while she was pregnant. So, she stayed at my apartment in Salem [Massachusetts], while I was living at the house doing this."

I was thrilled for Hanson. He had everything in place that summer, between a baby on the way, the new house, and a recent pivot in his career. He was launching that unique phase in adulthood when "living a full life" really takes on meaning and makes sense. I realize having children is not for everyone, nor is owning a home. But for me, that's when I began to really understand what my full life looked like—finding the right balance of family, work, and fun as I define each of them. That summer, I felt Hanson was discovering this as well. Of course, I was also hoping he would join me on the Jefferson hike.

"I had already done Jefferson, but I was totally in when I saw your text. I knew I wanted to do them all again anyway," said Hanson. "But Hannah was like, 'You can't go hiking. You gotta finish painting the house.' But I was going and she was not happy. I told her I would paint this last room and do the hike in the same day. I drove up, met you, and we crushed it."

Hanson and I met at Foster's Crossroads in Twin Mountain. I left my car at the historic White Mountains landmark that was once the Rosebrook Inn and dated back more than 100 years. In the summer of 2022, Foster's was torn down, as the building was deemed unsafe. Foster's was not only popular for tourists, it was the ideal pre- and post-hike stop for those of us driving I-93 to or from Crawford Notch and Pinkham Notch who needed gas, Gatorade, and ice cream. As we made our way to the Caps Ridge Trailhead, I pitched Hanson on another idea, The Link Trail. This was consistent with our ongoing effort to "get the most bang for our buck."

I told him that, from everything I read, the trail was seldom used and would likely be gnarly, often tough to navigate. It might slow us down but it would give us a very cool loop, and another perspective of

Jefferson, the state's third biggest mountain. Plus, we would only be adding 1.6 miles onto the hike and we would get to summit Jefferson via the Castle Trail, which meant climbing over "The Castles," the killer rock formations along this route from which its name is derived. Looking back, I imagine I had him at, "I have an idea."

We parked at the lot along Jefferson Notch Road and made fast time getting on trail. We agreed, for the sake of our families, we would make an effort to move swiftly and keep the extracurriculars to a minimum. And we tried. We ripped out the first 1.1 miles up the Caps Ridge Trail, which got us to 3,800 feet and the junction of The Link. We took a left and started on the trail that the leading guide to hiking the NH 48, *The 4000-Footers of the White Mountains*, describes as "extremely rough and tiring, making for slow going." The Link stays in the forest during this stretch with the exception of a rockslide, which delivers great views. The 4000-Footers guide also reports The Link is "noted for treacherous footing with rocks, roots, and holes." We found all of this to be true and we loved it. The footing was indeed dangerous, and often sloped with unstable ground below our feet. It was just such a unique trail and that made it memorable, another real highlight to the NH 48 journey.

"The Link Trail was all roots and rocks with nothing underneath it supporting it," said Hanson. "You could break something. I did smash my tibia and it bled for a while. There's a photo of that somewhere."

We reached the junction of the Castle Trail at an elevation of 4,025 feet. We were essentially above treeline and staring straight up Castellated Ridge, another of the White Mountains' glorious features. We had 1.5 miles to reach the summit and the combination of the panoramic views and the upcoming rock "Castles" was quickly making this hike epic. In fact, the time spent on and around the Castles that day were as much fun as I've had on any rocks. Hanson and I kept calling Jefferson "El Jefe." We were alone on the ridge and repeating cries of, "To the summit. El Jefe we are coming for you." It was just part of that day's trail talk and it entertained us amid one of the most breathtaking sections of trail I have ever hiked.

We reached the summit of El Jefe (5,716 feet), had a quick lunch, and took some pictures. There were a few other folks on the peak, and they were summit squatting (the unhealthy practice of setting up camp on a mountain's summit, and by doing so, limiting other hikers' access to the highest point for photos and/or a moment to celebrate). This fueled us to keep on keepin' on. We moved quickly down the Caps Ridge Trail despite the amount of rock scrambling necessary. Make no mistake, and don't let the short distance fool you, Caps Ridge is a trail that needs to be respected and taken with caution. Yet, Hanson was all business, billy goating his way down. I knew he had a paintbrush waiting for him, while I was returning to a family vacation. At one point, he was way ahead of me and despite my efforts to make up time, I just don't move that fast. But his movement was halted soon after the junction to The Link Trail, when he reached the ledge featuring the Caps Ridge "potholes," another unique element to this hike. Hanson, a Fitchburg State-educated scientist, was fascinated with them and this allowed me to catch up. He explained how they were formed in great detail (melting glacial water and erosion) and was excited to do so. From here, we had just a mile back to the trailhead.

"That was another beautiful day," said Hanson. "We summited, came down the Caps Ridge Trail, got back to my car, and got back to Foster's. I drove home and painted that room. Hannah was still mad at me but it was worth it."

## CLIFF NOTES: WMS CHAPTER 10

🥾 There really is some value to taking the road, or trail, less traveled.

🥾 Don't underestimate family support, as it is imperative to achieving long-term hiking goals.

🥾 Understanding a hike means more than just learning the route; consider digging in on local history and a mountain's geological makeup.

**Facebook Post:**

 Keith Gentili
August 27, 2013

MOUNT JEFFERSON (5,716 ft.)—Spent a little time in Jefferson, NH, last week so it seemed natural to climb our state's 3rd highest peak. I'll add details in captions as this one had some very cool features. This marks No. 20 of 48 and my only Presidential except Washington.

# CHAPTER 11
# The Birthday Hike

Date: Friday, September 27, 2013
Mountain Range: Pemigewasset Wilderness
Peak/Elevation (feet): Hancock 4,420, South Hancock 4,319
Route (Lollipop): Hancock Notch to Cedar Brook to Hancock
  Loop to Cedar Brook to Hancock Notch
Total Distance: 9.8 miles
Hiking Partners: None
Road to 48: #21, #22

Unlike the July 31 Whiteface-Passaconaway solo hike that sort of just happened, the plan to summit the Hancocks alone on Friday, September 27, 2013, was on the schedule for the entire month. That date was my 46th birthday and I was taking a personal day to go hiking, and more specifically, solo hiking. It was something I wanted to do as I knew the Fitchburg State Hiking Club was going to reassemble in October to close out the season, just as we did during "Freshman Year." I wanted another solo hike as an "underclassman" because there still were lessons I felt I needed, including solo night hiking, and this was that opportunity.

The Hancocks also represented the last of the NH 48 southern mountains for me. After this hike, my attention would be shifting north toward Crawford Notch and Pinkham Notch. That meant considerably longer drives to trailheads and the need to schedule bigger hiking windows. But that was always the plan. I knew that as the 2014 hiking season began, my commitment would have to increase as I would be closer to the end of the NH 48 than I was to the start. At this moment, prior to summiting the Hancocks, I was at 20/48 and feeling on schedule. The Hancocks would get me to 22 and, with the October hike—Tom, Field, and Willey—already on the calendar, I was slated to finish 2013 at 25/48.

I got my typical late departure from New Boston on my birthday, ultimately hitting the road around 12:30pm. I was beginning to settle into a routine that included a gas stop at the Cumberland Farms in Goffstown as well as a supplies (food/drink) stop at the local grocery store, Sully's. My go-to snacks were becoming Kind Bars, Clif Bars, and Snickers, and I would typically try a random energy bar that was on sale or a unique flavor. Although, I had trouble saying no to any combination of chocolate and peanut butter from any of the snack makers. Sully's also offered premade sandwiches with cool names and these started to become my regular hiking lunches. My staple throughout the NH 48 was The Grizzly, which includes roast beef and a horseradish mayo. The Pilgrim was a close second thanks to its turkey, cranberry sauce, and stuffing.

These two stops pushed my arrival time at the Hancock Overlook, which is just east of the hairpin turn on the Kancamagus Highway, to 2:30pm. After stretching out and gearing up, I was on trail by 3pm at an elevation of 2,129 feet. This ensured that I would enjoy Golden Hour (sunset was scheduled for 6:30pm) on trail as well as solo night hiking my way back to the car.

The Hancock Loop Trail is a lollipop hike. The distance, or stick, to reach the loop is 3.6 miles and it includes three sections. The first 1.8 miles along the Hancock Notch Trail is nearly flat and was knocked off pretty quickly. At the junction of the Cedar Brook Trail (2,520 feet), I turned left onto it. The next .7 miles featured a few water crossings and little more elevation gain as I reached the Hancock Loop Trail at 2,720 feet. The next 1.1 miles got me to the intersection of the North and South Links of the Hancock Loop Trail. Here, I was 3.6 miles from the trailhead and at an elevation of 3,600 feet. I chose to go left and climb North Hancock first. This is the more common approach due to the section of the trail that lay ahead, .6 miles with 1,020 feet of vertical gain.

So, like climbing the North Slide on the Tripyramids, the Flume Slide, and East Osceola, this hike features another very steep section to reach the peak. But I was excited. I felt strong. The hike was going well and I was ready to put a summit push on. And I did. I began climbing and I was feeling it, in a good way. I was sweating heavily and trying to take big steps up. I was in it, and then I heard my cell phone start lighting up. It was so strange to be working my way up the side of that mountain, and in that moment of really grinding out elevation, have my phone go off.

78

It was quickly obvious that I had hit a reception hot spot. The series of texts pinging and popping was unmistakable. I couldn't stop myself from digging out my iPhone. Thus, I made the call to take a seat right there on the side of North Hancock. Although the business day was kind of over, as it was after 5pm, it was still a workday. I decided I would, at the least, put a read on things and digest what came in. Maybe somebody needed me. At this time in my career, I was in year 10 of being a minority owner of a small business that specialized in making officially licensed sports and concert ticket-related products and displays. As I was reading my messages, I was also hydrating and fueling up. It just made sense. I was multi-tasking. Then, my phone rang. Ugh.

I could see it was the Boston Red Sox. Well, it was my contact at the Red Sox team store, a key customer. Despite chomping on a Kind Bar, buried in sweat, and at an elevation of 4,000 feet, I took the call. I knew it was important as the Red Sox had recently clinched the 2013 American League East Division and were headed to the Major League Baseball (MLB) playoffs. This call was the first step in discussions that, if the Red Sox were to advance to the World Series, my company (That's My Ticket) would want to be on site at Fenway Park selling product. It was a successful program we launched in the summer of 2008 at Yankee Stadium for the MLB All-Star Game and took to Citizens Bank Park in Philadelphia for the 2008 World Series. The call went well and it put a little hop in my step as I got back on trail.

I churned out the final ascent to the summit of North Hancock (4,420 feet). I felt really good. The weather was nice and I had just completed the heavy lifting for this hike. I was sure to enjoy the big open view to the south from the overlook for a bit. Also, I had recently purchased ($4.99) the app "PeakFinder" and I was anxious to use it at this elevation. PeakFinder identifies mountains by simply opening the app and pointing your phone at mountains. It really helped me, as I was not good at identifying mountains whether I had climbed them or not. Plus, there are more than 700 peaks in the White Mountains, so trying to recognize any of them was always difficult for me. On this day atop North Hancock, PeakFinder taught me that I was staring right at the Osceolas. That was very satisfying, as I had climbed them in May. The NH 48 puzzle was coming together.

I made my way across the Hancock Ridge 1.4 miles to the summit of South Hancock. It's an easy hike through the woods and there's a little reward as South Hancock offers a view. It was early fall, and the sun was falling as I stood here. Although both peaks were now attained, I needed to return to my car safely on foot for the AMC to count them and I still had 4.1 miles remaining. So, I got after it and began to descend the South Link. I made pretty good work of this section (.5 miles) and got down to the intersection with the North Link quickly. I continued to churn out the remainder of the Hancock Loop Trail as the evening light dissipated.

I recalled my discussion with Hanson on Tecumseh about not going to my headlamp too soon. I had purchased a new headlamp since that hike too. I bought the Petzl Tikka for about $30 at Eastern Mountain Sports and it was serving me well. But I chose to not put it on early. At the very least I wanted to traverse the .7 miles of the Cedar Brook Trail and reach the Hancock Notch Trail before lighting up. It's little mind games like this that hikers often play while solo hiking, to help us further down the trail for stretches at a time. I did make it to the Hancock Notch Trail before turning on my headlamp.

It was 1.8 miles from there to return to the Hancock Overlook. I was on the homestretch with about an hour remaining on trail. Outside of my headlamp's range, it was pitch black. I found myself hiking oddly faster, not because I was in a rush but because I was getting anxious. I soon started hearing everything, which only fed my anxiety. It wasn't long before I thought I was being followed or stalked. By what? I wasn't sure but, in my mind that evening, the two leading candidates were another person or a bear. Yep, it was happening. I was starting to panic a bit and I'm not sure why. It wasn't even on my radar—the idea that I would, in essence, be spooked on the trail while night hiking solo. I had done this numerous times dating back to my Virginia years.

I opted to put my head down and focus on the ground ahead of me. I continued to move briskly, stepping into my headlamp's circle of light. Right foot, left foot. Eventually, I heard a car traveling along the Kancamagus Highway and it instantly calmed me. That was all it took to bring me down. The sound of the car represented that I was no longer in the woods, or alone. I was able to finish the final piece of trail walking leisurely out. I got to my car, which was alone in the parking lot, and allowed myself a few minutes of decompressing the events of my birthday hike before starting the drive home. To this day, I have never experienced anything like that moment on trail, and I have done a lot of night hiking over the years, solo as well as with others.

"I hiked alone a lot during the New Hampshire 48. When alone, you start thinking about what's important to you," said Engler. "And it always comes back to family. Your family is what's important."

I agree with Engler's assessment. Yet, on the Hancock hike, once I got it in my mind that I was possibly being followed, I couldn't shake the idea of it. It trumped everything. Although, on some level, I think I knew I wasn't being followed. Yet, there I was, nearly trail running my way back to my car.

"Hannah was always nervous about me hiking solo, but she trusted me. She trusted me to not to do anything dumb or get myself in any trouble," said Hanson. "When you're at the top of a mountain, or in the woods, and you are really alone, there's something very spiritual about that. It is just you and whatever sounds surround you. But it can also be very lonely."

## CLIFF NOTES: WMS CHAPTER 11

🏃 When you reach a spot at altitude with cell reception, do not instantly grab for your phone. Get to your next safe spot before attempting to review any messages.

🏃 Schedule a solo hike and do the homework to maximize the experience.

🏃 The PeakFinder app, at $4.99, is a worthy investment for anyone interested in mountains.

🏃 Always pack a headlamp, regardless of when your hike starts, and consider turning it on after your eyes adjust to the night.

**Facebook Post:**

Keith Gentili
October 11, 2013

ROAD TO 48 (UPDATE)—September solo hike of the Hancocks included two peaks (North & South), 9.8 miles, just 2,700 feet in vertical gain and 5 hours on trail...the final hour or so in the dark by headlamp. That's 22 summits down, 26 to go. October target is Crawford Notch and Mts. Tom/Field/Willey.

# CHAPTER 12
# The Return of the
# Fitchburg State Hiking Club

Date: Sunday, October 27, 2013
Mountain Range: Willey
Peak/Elevation (feet): Willey 4,285, Field 4,340, Tom 4,051
Route (Thru Hike): Kedron Flume to Ethan Pond to Willey
  Range to A-Z to Mount Tom Spur to A-Z to Avalon
Total Distance: 8.5 miles
Hiking Partners: Eric Hanson, Eric Engler, Keith Rice
Road to 48: #23, #24, #25

Planning the Willey-Field-Tom hike was nearly as much fun as pulling it off. All four members of the Fitchburg State Hiking Club had signed on back in September so I had time to flesh out a variety of options. It was now almost Halloween and I hadn't been on trail with Rice or Engler since the Traverse of the Bonds, which was the weekend before Memorial Day. Plus, two of my last four hikes were solo adventures. So, in putting together the October plan, I knew I was looking for something a little more than the traditional Tom-Field-Willey route from the Crawford Depot to wrap up the 2013 hiking season.

"We were better prepared. Better gear. More learned by then," said Rice. "We had a better understanding of what we would get into and where we might run into it. 'Cause you never know. We knew once you are up there, life at elevation is different."

By this time, I had read a lot about Crawford Notch and the many options for hiking these mountains. Of particular interest to me was the Willey House and its family's tragic history. Samuel Willey, his wife Polly Lovejoy, their five children, and two workers were killed fleeing an 1826 landslide. However, their home—the Willey House, which sits essentially in the center of Crawford Notch—remained intact. It is believed that had the family sought shelter at home, they would have all survived.

I became drawn to this story's irony as well as the Kedron Flume, which includes a waterfall with a visible 150-foot drop that sits less than a mile behind the house. The attraction of these two features convinced me that this hike needed to start at the Willey House. It was somewhat unconventional but it wouldn't be that long (8.5 miles) if completed as I envisioned.

"We were fully established at this point," said Hanson. "I remember all of it. For me, driving up with Riceman, it was one of those trips where I felt like, yeah, we are a hiking club. We are all doing this together, again. All four of us. We are all in. We had a plan. It was a team. We spotted a car."

The plan did indeed mean spotting a car at the Crawford Depot. We would depart from the Willey House using the Kedron Flume Trail and then connect, briefly, to the Ethan Pond Trail before continuing on the Willey Range Trail. We would get to climb the famous Willey ladders and summit Willey first, before continuing on to Field and then Tom. It was another example of trying to find the biggest adventure. However, it was not the simple route as we were launching this hike from the floor of Crawford Notch (elevation 1,300 feet) and finishing at its top—Crawford Depot (elevation 1,900 feet).

"While driving up with Riceman, and even talking on the phone coordinating it beforehand, we both were saying, 'Why are we starting at the bottom?' But we knew you always wanted the most bang for the buck," Hanson told me. "It was the way of the Fitchburg State Hiking Club, looking to crush it. We were going to go the hard way and give you a hard time about it. We always gave you a hard time just to give you a hard time. We ragged on you for your enthusiasm."

It's true. We all met early that morning at Willey House before spotting my car up at the depot. It cost us a little time, maybe 15 minutes, and I got a nice wave of grief for it. Of course, that always started from the moment we got together anyway, so I was used to it. Looking back, I even enjoyed it, as it was part of the overall adventure.

It was chilly that morning, with some fog. We thought we might see some weather. It was quickly apparent, standing in the Willey House parking lot, that we were likely to get some precipitation, snow or rain or a combination of both. And that was just fine for all of us, even Engler who often could have a slightly different agenda.

"I was focused on catching up with the dudes as opposed to

memory making," said Engler. "It does sometimes aggravate me that I can't put some of the pieces together. Perhaps it's because I've been mentally declining for years now. Or it's just some kind of memory issue. Or maybe it's just not that important to me, some of those details. I don't really know."

We set out on the Kedron Flume Trail and it got steep fast. There are some switchbacks to help traverse up this side of the mountain and we arrived at the waterfall quickly. It being late October, there wasn't much action here and I took a nice round of heat for choosing this route to see the waterfall with barely any water falling. Ha.

We pushed on and met up with the Ethan Pond Trail at 1.3 miles and an elevation of 2,400 feet. Another .3 miles put us on the Willey Range Trail as we continued to work our way toward our first summit. The climb is legit. We were gaining elevation throughout and as we passed the two-mile mark, we were at 3,000 feet. Another half-mile or so and we arrived at the ladders. Built in 2004 by the AMC folks, 11 sections of ladders combine to move hikers up 100 feet in elevation (from 3,400 to 3,500).

"Those ladders made that section easy," said Rice. "But they were also covered in snow and treacherous at times."

"It was a challenge. As a group we were fine, but I was not ready for solo hiking something like that," said Engler. "Individually, I would not have been fine on the Willey-Field-Tom hike."

As we made our way up the ladders, we got our first White Mountains visit from a gray jay. Also known as a Canada Jay, these birds are notorious for befriending hikers in an effort to be fed a bit of trail mix, granola bar, or anything else folks might share with them especially from their hands. And on this day, it marked my first interaction with them on the NH 48 journey. Like so many hikers who came before and after, by the time we reached the summit of Willey (4,285 feet), we had a little posse of gray jays traveling with us.

"It was frosty on the summit and the gray jay show was great. You guys had never seen them before and were so enamored with them," said Hanson. "That was the first time for you guys feeding the gray jays."

I am guilty of feeding a gray jay. But I knew feeding wildlife wasn't a good idea; I really did it for my daughters. This is not an excuse, just the truth. I just thought they would get such a kick out of watching the video. For the Bonds traverse, I had kidnapped one of my daughter Julia's stuffed animals. This little dachshund named Weenie, who was sort of my nemesis during those years. While I threatened to do bad things to Weenie via texts to my family, in the end, he got a 20-mile ride through the heart of the Pemigewasset Wilderness. I took pictures along the way and there's a great photo of Weenie sitting on my head at the summit of Mount Guyot (see page 56). As I stood on the Willey summit overlook and held out a small piece of bread from my sandwich, I was still not sure I wanted to do it. Then, a gray jay launched off a nearby pine branch and came at me. I flinched, hard.

"You tease," said Engler. "You're a tease."

This can be heard on the video Engler shot of me holding my hand out. That same jay quickly circled around and made a second run. This time I held my position firm and it took the food from my hand. Hanson lets out a celebratory, "There it is," as the jay scores its snack.

"The backdrop of that video is the classic snow-capped Presidentials," said Hanson. "Webster, Jackson, up to Pierce, up to Washington in the frost."

"I was floored by that," said Engler of the gray jay experience. "I was just blown away by that."

In addition to lunch and playing with birds, we also celebrated our first peak by resting up. It was a nice reward for the nearly 3,000 feet of elevation that we climbed during the hike's first 2.7 miles. We certainly were not in a hurry to start the 1.4-mile trek to Mount Field.

"The views were just so spectacular that day from Willey," said Hanson. "Washington and the Presidentials. Just so great."

Rice agreed. "What a great view across Crawford Notch," he said. "That up-close view of the Presidentials. Just awesome."

As we began to make our way over to Field, it started snowing. Lightly, but it continued long enough that the trail and its surroundings got a clean white blanket. The result was breathtaking. The four of us were now four miles in, about to hit our second summit, and just having a ball in a freshly made winter wonderland. When we reached the viewless summit of Field (4,340 feet), there was another group of hikers hanging out. Engler asked them if they would take a group picture. They obliged, of course, and did so by snapping two shots. The images from these photos capture the Fitchburg State Hiking Club at a real high, standing amid a snowcapped Narnia-like setting.

"I'm wearing my heavy cotton Mets sweatshirt in those photos," said Engler.

Hanson recalls it as well. "Engler's wearing his Mets cotton hoody but we are killing it. We were on a quest, like Fellowship of the Ring-type stuff that day. Our 48 journey was happening."

From the Field summit, we descended the final mile of the Willey Range Trail to the junction of the A-Z trail, and 3,700 feet. Here, we took the A-Z Trail for just a moment (100 yards) and turned left on the Mount Tom Spur Trail. This would be our final climb of the day, .9 miles and 351 feet. We churned it out only to find the summit of Tom socked in. But while there were no views, we did get some more gray jay action. By now, though, we were on to their game. We also got a little hail as temperatures were dropping.

"It was so foggy on Tom," said Engler. "I've said it before, that feeling I get when getting to the top, and I recognized it later, how I'm feeling, the pacing and my heart rate going up. I had enough challenges with gear, etc., that holding on to the memories wasn't a primary focus. We didn't really have the gear then like we did later. We didn't have Microspikes yet, or the ideal layers of clothing."

After summiting Tom, it was all downhill. We made our way down the spur trail and picked up the A-Z Trail. After another mile, we continued straight on the Avalon Trail. This left just 1.3 miles to reach the Crawford Depot. We made pretty quick work of it all and loaded right into my car. After 8.5 miles and 3,600 total feet of elevation gain, we were all business and headed back to the Willey House.

Why? Well, the Boston Red Sox had advanced to the 2013 World Series and first pitch of Game 4 was scheduled that night for 8:17pm local time (7:17pm in St Louis). We started early that morning so that we'd get back to see if the Red Sox could even the series at two. They did. In fact, the Red Sox would also win Game 5 in St. Louis the next night to take a 3-2 series lead. This meant the scene was shifting to Boston's Fenway Park on October 30 for Game 6. I was fortunate to be in the building that night, working the That's My Ticket product booth for most of the game. However, I did get to my seat for the final three outs as the Red Sox won their eighth World Series championship. It was a great experience, just as the Willey-Tom-Field hike had been three days earlier.

"That was a good day; a great hike," said Rice. "It snowed on us for a bit. It didn't last all day, just flurries for a while. That added something. I slept on the way home."

---

**CLIFF NOTES: WMS CHAPTER 12**

🥾 Spotting a car at the end of the trailhead for a thru hike is always a strategy worth exploring.

🥾 Feeding wildlife, regardless of how entertaining it is in the moment, is not a good idea.

🥾 Being in your favorite team's home stadium for a championship-clinching moment is more emotional and special than expected.

---

**Facebook Post:**

Keith Gentili
October 29, 2013

ROAD TO 48 UPDATE—Got out on Sunday and hit the Crawford Notch Trifecta of Mt. Willey, Mt. Field, and Mt. Tom. Nice mix of hail and fresh snow. Total hike: 8.5 miles, 7.5 hours, 3,600 feet of elevation gain. That's 25 down, 23 to go...in golf terms, that's making the turn/welcome to the back 9.

# 2014
# JUNIOR YEAR
# PEAKS #26–39

# CHAPTER 13
## Enter Snowshoes

Date: Saturday-Sunday, April 5-6, 2014
Mountain Range: Pilot
Peak/Elevation (feet): Cabot 4,170
Route (Out and Back): York Pond to Bunnell Notch to Kilkenny
  Ridge
Total Distance: 9.4 miles
Hiking Partners: Eric Hanson, Eric Engler, Keith Rice
Road to 48: #26

During the winter of 2013-2014, the Fitchburg State Hiking Club developed quite the itch to get back on trail. By March, the four of us—Hanson, Engler, Rice, and I—began discussing plans for the season's first hike. We were looking to get out early and go big. We agreed on April 5, which was three full weeks earlier than the previous year's opening hike (Tecumseh, Chapter 5). We chose Mount Cabot, the northernmost peak of the NH 48. And we committed to doing it as an overnight hike as Cabot has a small, two-room cabin on it that features four bunks.

"Elsa was born on March 16. I really didn't know if I could do a hike that early," said Hanson. "But I was still reading all the planning texts. I jumped in at one point and said, 'Do you guys have snowshoes? You're going to need them.'"

Engler and Rice, like Hanson, owned snowshoes. I did not. In fact, I had never strapped on a pair of snowshoes in my adult life ("And now you're going to climb a 4,000-foot mountain in them," said Hanson). Yet, I was thrilled, as it felt like a natural evolution in extending the hiking calendar. Rice borrowed a pair from his neighbor for me and the Cabot quest was officially on. I was confident that we were going to snowshoe up this mountain and have a blast doing it.

"Hanson and Engler both had snowshoes with the heel lifts," Rice told me. "Ours didn't. We had cross-country style. They had alpine shoes."

Hanson's snowshoes were essentially brand new. Hannah bought them for him that Christmas after his previous pair gave out on a Mount Hedgehog hike they were doing together. Although he hadn't been able to commit to this trip, I got the sense he hadn't given up on it either.

"Then, one day, my wonderful wife said, 'Those guys are going, you can go too. Just come home at night,'" said Hanson. "I was like, 'Really? I can do that.' I didn't care how hard it was going to be or how long it was going to take me to get back. I was in."

Engler, too, was all in. But as he had said before, the mountain and the conditions had nothing to do with his decision.

"I knew my buddies were going hiking and I wanted to go with them. It was pure FOMO, fear of missing out," said Engler. "But what was different about the Cabot hike is that it wasn't a day hike. On this one, I'd have to see what I could fit into my overnight pack."

The morning of Saturday, April 5, the four of us traveled in three cars and met in New Hampshire's North Country. We were headed to the Unknown Pond parking area, which is just past the Berlin Fish Hatchery off Bog Dam Road.

"It was still a winter wonderland up there on April 5. Everything was covered in snow," said Rice. "We were concerned about the road conditions going into the fish hatchery. We saw some ducks in a pond and there was snow right up to the edge of it and some ice. They were sort of just sitting in the middle of it."

Added Hanson, "We got to the trailhead and there was a couple of feet of snow. Good thing we all had snowshoes."

So, we all strapped them on right there for the start of the hike. They were necessary and it was advantageous, especially for me, to begin finding my stride (or gait) with fresh legs. As a group, it was also obvious that our packs would be fully loaded.

"This was my 14th 4,000-footer and I still really didn't know what I was doing. But I figured I'd just follow you guys," said Engler. "The problem was I didn't have enough experience to really have a handle on modern equipment, clothing, or technology. I packed way too heavy in preparation for not knowing what the conditions would be when we got up there."

One item Engler had, which may sound excessive in terms of backpacking, turned out to play a big role in the trip. He brought a small camping heater called the Little Buddy. Available from REI for about $100, he had that and a propane tank with him at the trailhead.

"But I couldn't carry it. My pack was too heavy," said Engler. "So I asked Hanson and he said yes."

Rice agreed, "We had a ton of gear. I had a second propane tank and Engler also had a torch."

We started on the York Pond Trail at an elevation of 1,670 feet. We were moving just fine out of the gate. At .2 miles, we bore right onto the Bunnell Notch Trail. There was a monorail to trek along and, at this point, any weather that was coming was holding off. We could tell something was brewing, but for now, we had a chance to work out any kinks.

"Even on the monorail with our snowshoes, we were post-holing a bit," said Rice. "We had to be careful to stay centered."

We had a few brook crossings that also provided some challenges, but otherwise we were getting down the trail okay. We saw a marten in a tree, which marked our first NH 48 wildlife sighting since a grouse on the Bonds traverse (Chapter 7).

Around the two-mile mark (2,300 feet), the trail started to climb. We felt it. By the three mile mark, we were at 3,040 feet and the grind was on. The combination of our pack weight, inexperience on snowshoes, and the now-falling snow meant we were in for a slog the rest of the way to the Cabot Cabin, which sat 4.4 miles from the parking area and at an elevation of 4,070 feet.

"We all began to climb at our own speed and we got separated on the way up at this point," said Rice. "I remember standing in the snow and thinking how bad my ankles were doing. My legs were burnt. I took my pack off and ate a few candy bars. I needed some fuel to help me on the rest of the way up."

Engler was also feeling the challenge.

"It was a direct hike up; we didn't stop to enjoy the view or eat and it was snowing a lot. I got very hungry on that hike. I was by myself at that point but I wasn't going to stop. I just wanted to try to keep up with the group," said Engler. "Snowshoeing and not being in shape and not stopping on the way up as we usually did, made it a tough climb."

Hanson and Rice did get ahead of Engler and me on the ascent. That was not uncommon based solely on our regular hiking speed. Those two just move a bit faster on trail, which is fine. As I reached Bunnell Rock (3,350 feet) at 3.8 miles, my legs began to tell me they were almost done. When I was much heavier, some 30-40 pounds heavier than I was on this day, my legs often cramped on big hikes—something I pointed out in the Orientation regarding my Mount Washington climb. It also happened twice in 1999, on my second climb of Maine's Katahdin and on Mount Greylock in Massachusetts. I learned how to combat cramps. That wasn't the case this time. My legs weren't cramping; they were just tired and starting to get weak.

To reach the Cabot Cabin, the final stretch of trail is basically flat. As I made my way toward it, I got my first case of the jelly legs. Both of them were just shaking and trembling with every step and continued to do so right to the cabin's front door. Three years later, on February 19, 2017, after 13 miles over 11 hours of snowshoeing up and down Mount Isolation, I got my second case of the jelly legs trying to walk into Moat Mountain Brewing Company in North Conway for a post-hike meal. It transported me right back to Cabot. Hanson and Rice were already at the cabin sporting big smiles. Engler was behind me.

"Eventually, I was just starving. I had to take my pack off and eat something," said Engler. "I had some beef jerky. As I put my pack back on, I took a step out from behind a tree and I could see the cabin."

With all four us now together at our destination, we couldn't help but feel a sense of accomplishment. It had been snowing for a while and the wind was really beginning to pick up. We took some pictures and shot some video. It was a celebration. Engler, Rice, and I went into the cabin to get set up for the night.

"I made a run for the summit," said Hanson, who was on the clock to depart. "I made it about a quarter of a mile or so but bailed. I opted to return to the cabin where you guys were pouring drinks and getting the place warm."

Said Rice, "We didn't even consider summiting that night. We got to the cabin and it was cold and snowing, and the wind was

blowing. We were hungry and thirsty and knew we'd do it the next day."

Engler fired up his Little Buddy heater and began to weatherproof the place. He was determined to get that cabin warm and had a plan.

"I brought up a roll of two-inch, black-paper tape from work. The windows were cracked, and it was cold in there. I sealed them up," said Engler. "I hung a poncho over the door and taped that up. I hung a tarp between the rooms. The plan was to heat each room while we were in it. I also taped up the stovepipe. The stove was taken out for safety a while ago but the vent was still there. I taped it so our heat wouldn't blow up it."

Rice and I were in the kitchen area, taking inventory on food, beverages, and assembling the evening's menu. With all the fresh snow, we knew we had endless amounts of water to use for mixed drinks and cooking. Good things were happening.

"We had both powders and squirts to make mixed drinks," said Rice. "We were scooping snow and making slushies."

Engler reminded me, "I brought two 32-ounce Coke bottles pre-mixed with 94-proof rum. And you kept poo-pooing them on the way up. You just kept saying 'When did you make them? They're going to be flat. Those won't be any good.' But they were great and you loved them."

With our encouragement and support, Hanson went into pure recreation mode as he had the biggest task ahead of him.

"I just worked on getting some rest," said Hanson. "And getting warm before heading down."

Said Engler, "It was snowing and cold. The sun was going down and Hanson had to make that return hike down on his own. At that time, I still felt I was a novice and I couldn't have done that. I thought it was crazy. He was very confident in himself, but it caught me off guard a bit that Hanson was going to hike down on his own right then."

The four of us really had some fun during that first hour or so upon reaching the cabin. Along with our drinks, we had a nice spread of appetizers including shrimp, trail mix, jerky, as well as crackers and cheese. We were in just such great spirits having conquered our first 4,000-foot peak in snowshoes. All was right.

"Then Hanson was like, 'I have to go,'" said Rice.

"I gave him my Black Diamond, size-large gloves," said Engler. "They were awesome, form-fitting gloves. They made your hands form into the shape of the gloves. They were waterproof and he wore them down."

It was an interesting moment on top of Cabot, amid the wind and snow. Part of me was concerned for Hanson's safety, of course, but part of me was caught up in the celebration that had just exploded. We were still whooping it up as he was packing up. There are some great pictures and videos of Hanson's departure. Just before he left, with snowshoes and pack on, he ripped out an air-guitar solo for the ages using a hiking pole as his guitar. Then, he was gone.

Here is Hanson's story of his descent and subsequent drive home, in his own words.

"It was squally on the way down. I got a couple of twilight views but it was getting dark and cold. At some point, I figured out that I put my new snowshoes on the wrong feet. I didn't even know there was a left and right because my old ones weren't like that. As I got near the bottom, as I got more tired, I started tripping on them. There just wasn't much gas left in my tank. I would trip, fall, and get up.

"At the bottom of the hike, on the last 100 yards or so to the car, which was totally flat, I fell and just laid there in the snow thinking I couldn't make it. I didn't have the strength to get up. It took me a good five minutes or so to get up that final time to get to the car. It must have been around 11pm. Then, I had to drive home and we were way up north.

"I got on the road and I had to pull my Hannaford move. The Hannaford [supermarket] in Ossipee was my nap spot. I pulled in that parking lot and got a little sleep. I finally got home around 3am, went to bed, and Elsa woke up. Hannah rolled over and said, 'It's your turn to feed the baby,' and I did. The next day I found out that I ruined my new snowshoes by whacking them all the way down."

Back at the cabin, things were heating up including the front room in which we were hanging out, as well as the first course of our supper.

"Rice cooked the dinner, some dehydrated meals, and you were complaining about the cheese in the lasagna," Engler told me. "You kept saying, 'This isn't right. It doesn't taste right. There's something wrong. The cheese tastes off.' I kept saying, 'It's fine. Stop complaining. What's wrong with you?' Then, we checked the date on the packaging and it had expired two years ago. You were right."

Of course, we had plenty of other meals to cook and nobody went hungry. We just had to run outside to scoop more snow every so often to melt for water to keep the kitchen engine running. We also set up a makeshift clothesline to dry our wet clothes. We really did get comfortable in there and were in no rush for the night to end. But...

"We drank everything we had and went to bed," said Rice. "The bunks had foam sleeping pads stapled down, built right into them. When we threw our own stuff down, we got really comfortable. Plus, we had the heater going in there now."

The bunks in the cabin were long and wide. After snowshoeing more than four miles and climbing nearly 3,000 feet of elevation, we were going to get a good night's sleep. The heater ensured that by taking the chill out of the room.

"Riceman got up in the middle of the night," said Engler. "And he knocked the heater over and it shut off. So, when we woke up it was freezing in that room."

Rice admitted to this but added that it may have been a good thing.

"Yeah, I bumped the thing and it had a great shut-off mechanism. It went off and I was fine with that," he said. "We were warm in our beds. The next morning, we had propane left so we could fire it up and have heat in the morning. We had heat while making breakfast and packing up."

It's true. Had Rice not bumped the Little Buddy, we would not have had any heat in the morning. The final propane tank would have just run out.

"In the morning, you were mad because your pants were cold," Rice told me. "You hated putting them on. They were basically frozen stiff. Engler and I both said, 'Why didn't you put them in your sleeping bag?' You were like, 'I didn't know about that.'"

In addition to a little heat and breakfast, the morning also brought blue skies. The storm that raged all night was gone.

"I recall the wind was blowing 40 to 60 miles per hour during the overnight with gusts up to 80 miles per hour. But I remember how beautiful it was the next day," said Engler. "When we left the cabin and went up in elevation in search of the summit and were on top of the snowpack, the view was just outstanding. We wouldn't have had the view if it wasn't for the snow. We were looking out over the trees. You can see it in the pictures. That was crazy to me. It was a new experience. Standing atop all that snow, seeing over the tops of the trees."

"It was a gorgeous morning," said Rice. "We had a great view of the Presidential Range. It was just perfect."

After summiting, the three of us began our trek down. It was going to be nearly a five-mile snowshoe out, reversing our route from the previous day.

"The hike out was a piece of cake because of our light packs. We ate and drank everything," said Rice. "I will say the next time I went up a mountain on snowshoes I had MSR Ascents, great shoes for climbing."

The Cabot Cabin treated the Fitchburg State Hiking Club better than I could have ever imagined. In fact, it over-delivered as we had so much fun up there. To say we bonded, or had a special moment, wouldn't be fair because we were already close. However, it was our first real winter adventure together and our trust in one another certainly strengthened. It was undeniable.

"That was one of the better hikes I've been on," said Engler. "And it was an overnighter, which is not really my thing, but that was so great. You can see in the photos and videos just how much fun we were having. It was nothing but good times. There was limited stress knowing we were going to hike down with nearly empty packs the next day."

Said Hanson. "That's the biggest hike and mountain I'd done on snowshoes to that point. And the Cabot Cabin is one of the best shelters in the White Mountains."

A few weeks after the Cabot trip, Engler got into a conversation at work and the White Mountains came up.

"I know a guy at work who is a hiker," said Engler. "We were talking not too long after this trip and he said he had just gone up Cabot. I said, 'I just hiked Cabot, too.' I told him about our trip and he said he recognized the black-paper tape from our job. That was very funny to me."

## CLIFF NOTES: WMS CHAPTER 13

🏃 Practice with new equipment. Take it out for a test run.

🏃 Check the expiration dates on your food. Don't waste critical pack space on food you can't eat.

🏃 Melt snow for water to cook and hydrate with. You can also add powders and squirts to it for flavor.

🏃 In winter conditions, keep yourself warm by filling your water bottle with hot water and placing it in your sleeping bag.

🏃 Keep your clothes warm by stuffing them in your sleeping bag at night.

---

**Facebook Post:**

Keith Gentili
April 6, 2014

ROAD TO 48 UPDATE (Mt. Cabot, 4,170)—Snowshoed up Mt. Cabot yesterday and slept on top in Cabot Cabin amid 60-80 mph winds and lots of snow. Woke to a clear day for descent; total trip 10 miles, 2,600 feet elevation gain. 26 down; 22 to go.

# CHAPTER 14
## Falling Down

Date: Sunday, May 4, 2014
Mountain Range: Pliny
Peak/Elevation (feet): Waumbek 4,006
Route (Out and Back): Starr King
Total Distance: 7.2 miles
Hiking Partners: Eric Hanson, Keith Rice
Road to 48: #27

The success of the April 5 Cabot trip was undeniable. My NH 48 journey had momentum and although the calendar confirmed it wasn't officially a winter hike, I knew that we had conquered extreme winter conditions. In fact, the combination of the first summit via snowshoes and rocking the Cabot Cabin overnight had my confidence at a new high. Perhaps that just came with the territory of being an "upperclassman." After all, it was 2014 and I was at 26/48.

Up next, Waumbek. It was only natural to wipe out the two North Country peaks back to back. I targeted Sunday, May 4, as both Hanson and Rice were available. I also liked the symmetry of completing these two mountains on 4/5 and 5/4, respectively. In planning the trip, we discussed snowshoes, and while we agreed we would see snow, the reports I was seeing on Facebook indicated they wouldn't be needed. There just wasn't that much snowpack remaining and we wouldn't be going above treeline.

The three of us met at the Starr King trailhead (elevation 1,600 feet), just off Route 2 in Jefferson and up the street from Santa's Village. It was a cold spring morning, and as we made our way up the leaf-covered trail, two hikers were coming down. But they didn't look like they had been hiking very long and it was clear they weren't returning from the summit. It was just too early.

"The father-son team," said Rice. "The son was like, 'If you don't have Microspikes, you won't make it to the summit.' The father was like, 'Well, maybe you can.'"

Added Hanson, "They did warn us. They were coming down. They said, 'We went up, hit ice, turned around, and came back. So, you really might not want to go up there. Do you have spikes?' Spikes? What are you talking about? We're good. We'll be okay."

We did reflect briefly on the suggestion of needing "spikes," and exactly what that meant. We knew what crampons were and we had just summited Cabot on snowshoes. Thus, the three of us felt that, combined, we had an understanding of winter traction. However, the term Microspikes was new to us. We continued up the trail.

The Starr King Trail climbs very gradually/moderately and is very straight. It continues this way for about two miles as it makes its way to the Mount Starr King summit at 2.6 miles and 3,907 feet. It was during this stretch that we encountered ice on the trail for the first time. At the lower elevation, the ice was spotty and we proceeded with caution.

"We could get over and around that early ice. There were rocks to step on," said Hanson. "Sort of like crossing a river. Rock hopping. It was manageable."

As we reached higher elevations, the ice was becoming more prevalent. Each of us were wearing hiking boots, but, as I soon came to learn, we were "barebooting." Meaning, we had no traction on over our boots. No snowshoes. No crampons. No Microspikes. And it was becoming a problem. We were starting to have trouble staying on the trail.

"Each one of us wiped out hard at some point," said Rice. "We were landing on our ass or on our knees and landing rough."

So much so, frustration was beginning to creep into the hike. This was new. There were moments on the Osceolas when I was post-holing, which included one of my barebooted feet busting through the trail's snowpack so that my leg essentially disappeared up to my knee and often my crotch. That was a lesson that led to the addition of snowshoes. This was worse. Not only was it mentally challenging, it was starting to feel dangerous. We were in a real battle.

"Then we hit those big ice flows that were coming down the mountainside, covering the entire trail and more," said Hanson. "And it became totally unmanageable."

It was during one of these ice flows that I began to lose the will to continue. I had gone down a few times in a row, on the same stretch of ice, and began to wonder if it was too risky to continue. I even said it aloud once to my hiking partners. They heard me, and calmed me down a bit.

"It was treacherous," said Rice. "This felt like it might be the one hike we need help getting off the hill."

Despite the conditions, the three of us, not surprisingly, agreed to push on. But I quickly took another hard fall. The trail was climbing and I was being careful, but it was pure ice. My feet just came out from under me and as I landed, I started to slide back down the trail.

"You were sliding down the mountain," Hanson told me. "I watched in horror and it was right after your meltdown. There was a downed spruce tree, just dead with the spikes coming out of it, like a medieval war device. I saw you sliding on your stomach and you were sliding right for it—I can still see it now. I was thinking, 'Oh my god, he's going to get impaled through his skull on this thing.' You kept sliding down and down and then you managed to stop yourself just before hitting it. It was then I realized, this is stupid, what are we doing?"

After my luge ride and near jousting, the three of us agreed to discuss the feasibility of this hike and if the Waumbek summit was still in our immediate future. In that moment, I didn't have much to offer. Admittedly, I was solely frustrated with the icy conditions and my own failure to navigate them. I had my hiking poles, something I added to my gear on the Bonds hike and had become accustomed to using. I believe they gave me a sort of four-wheel drive effect. But on this day, they were not a solution.

"We decided to abandon the trail, go into the forest, and use the base of the trees to step against and it changed our hike," said Rice. "We just had to keep the trail in sight and we were pretty much all set. The trees were also better to grab on to as hand holds rather than using hiking poles, as they were fixed."

Added Hanson, "The trail was so treacherous. But when we were able to go off trail, we could go tree to tree, like monkeys. It was still icy but there were pine needles on the surface of the ice that often gave us some grip. But really it was the trees that made the difference."

It worked. The three of us began moving slowly and somewhat steadily. It wasn't perfect and we did fall from time to time but the forest was a much safer environment to fall in than the trail.

"It was how we essentially got to the top of Starr King," said Rice. "We were able to stay about 15 feet off trail, higher up on the slope, in the trees, following the trail as much we could."

We reached the summit of Starr King (3,907 feet) without getting hurt. We were only 2.6 miles from the trailhead; yet, there was a real sense of achievement in the air as we knew our goal was now attainable, that we would indeed summit Waumbek. The possibility of turning around was real, and that makes this hike unique in its own way. There is certainly nothing wrong with changing the plan. It's a commonly accepted saying among hikers that the mountains aren't going anywhere. We can always come back another day.

"We were okay at that point, when we hit the Starr King summit and its chimney," said Hanson, of the brick chimney that greets hikers as the trail turns toward Waumbek. "Then it became more about just going across to the summit."

It was snowing at this point. There's a great photo of Rice and me standing in front of the chimney with big fluffy flakes falling. We had a mile left to our final destination and only 100 feet of elevation remaining. We ripped it out and saw moose tracks along the way. We also got a visit from a Canada (gray) jay. Once we arrived, we got busy setting up a tarp and essentially a lunch camp.

"We had a hot lunch and cold drinks," said Rice. "Hanson even said, 'We should be having hot drinks' not ice drinks. But we had ice. We were pouring a little honey whiskey over ice."

It's worth noting that on a winter hike of Mount Liberty a few years later (December 27, 2016), Hanson and I did indeed pull off Hot Toddies, complete with lemon juice and cloves. I believe the seed was planted for them atop Waumbek.

Added Hanson, "It was spitting snow and we had a great time. We had a hot lunch. You had the hamburger-macaroni-sauce thing again like on the Tripyramids."

We fueled up nicely on Waumbek. It was a very satisfying lunch, a celebration, and that made the trek down enjoyable. As we returned to the summit of Starr King on the way back, we broke into song:

*Starr King*

*You make my heart sing*

*You make everything groovy*

*Starr King*

*Starr King, I think I love you*

*But I wanna know for sure*

*So come on and hold me tight*

*I love you*


Of course, the music stopped when we hit the ice flows again. Yes, we were able to enter the woods and work ourselves from tree to tree, but it was still a challenge.

"Down wasn't as easy as up," said Rice. "Gravity was pulling us. Any misstep and we would slide even further. It happened to every one of us."

Said Hanson, "I was so bruised by the end of that hike. I went down so many times. Not just the flip up and fall, but also the full body slam down."

I also took one last big fall on the descent. It was a pure wipeout, as both feet went at the same time and came right out from under me together. I went up before coming straight down, landing on my ass and back. Although I didn't get seriously hurt, as I gathered myself together, I couldn't find one of my hiking poles.

"That's when you lost your pole. I love that story," said Hanson. "My kids get a kick out of that story. We looked for that thing for a while."

Said Rice, "We looked everywhere for your pole. For like five or 10 minutes. Three grown adults looking for a hiking pole. It shouldn't be this hard. I don't know why I finally looked up, but logic was telling me it's not on the ground. And there it was, dangling right above you in the branches of a pine tree."

Of course, it was above me…in a tree. It was just that kind of day, that kind of hike. My hiking poles were essentially all black. I changed the baskets to lime green after this so they would pop in nearly any condition: day, night, rain, or snow. It was a good decision, as I've had them come loose from me on a few occasions. This wasn't the only gear lesson of the day; I also researched and bought Kahtoola Microspikes soon after this hike. For $70, I never had to worry about ice again. Miscrospikes turned me into a billy goat on ice during the winter. In 2020, I bought a second pair.

"I never went on another winter hike again without Microspikes," said Rice.

The three of us continued to carry our sore bodies down the Starr King Trail that day. It was nearly dark when we reached the trailhead. We were the last ones off the mountain.

"When we got down to the bottom, we had a beer in the parking lot. It was like, damn, what a day, nice to be back down," said Hanson. "We hung out for a few minutes and said our goodbyes. Then, I got pulled over on the way home in Gorham, where the speed limit drops from 50 miles per hour to 35. I got nailed right there—a speeding ticket to end the day."

**Facebook Post:**

Keith Gentili
May 7, 2014

ROAD TO 48 UPDATE—While step-for-step it may have been the most dangerous hike I've been on, reaching the summit of Mt. Waumbek (4,006 feet) also made for great adventure. The trail featured about a mile of glacier-esque navigating and we weren't packing proper footwear (microspikes). So we slipped, fell, crashed, and bush-whacked to the top. Total trip: 7.2 miles, 2,700 feet of elevation gain, and lots of rain-snow-ice. 27 down; 21 to go.

# CHAPTER 15
# Staking a Claim

Date: Saturday, June 7, 2014
Mountain Range: Twin
Peak/Elevation (feet): Hale 4,054
Route (Thru Hike): Hale Brook to Lend-A-Hand to Ethan Pond
  to Zealand to Zealand Road
Total Distance: 8.7 miles
Hiking Partners: None
Road to 48: #28

Just as the success of April's overnight snowshoe hike to the Cabot Cabin delivered a big boost in my confidence, the epic failure navigating the never-ending ice on Mount Waumbek was a humbling reminder that there's always more to learn. In fact, I really chided myself for not getting educated on the entire product line of ice cleats, be it Microspikes or Yaktrax or whatever. Especially as I was now including early spring hiking conditions on my push to 48. Of course, as June rolled in, all thoughts of dealing with ice were gone as I shifted my focus to this month's hike, Mount Hale.

By now, my pre-hike research cycle was a well-oiled machine. I had my books and my maps, as well as a handful of websites bookmarked that I came to trust for updated trail descriptions and weather (see Resources, page 233). As I dug in on Hale, I noticed there was a certain lack of enthusiasm by many who climbed it. Much of this feedback was directed at the traditional route to the summit—the 4.4-mile out-and-back of the Hale Brook Trail. In short, I deduced from reviews and descriptions, the hike was going to be a bit of a snoozer. Well, this certainly did not match my philosophy of getting the most bang for my buck every time out. Thus, I chose to go bigger, and take the loop option noted on page 235 of *The 4000 Footers of the White Mountains* and visit Zealand Falls. This one decision changed everything. Now, I was getting 8.7 total miles on trail along with three big features—an AMC hut, waterfall, and pond—worth getting excited about.

I sent out the trip's itinerary, along with the usual invitation, and it became evident that none of my hiking partners were available. No problem. I mean it. I was good with this becoming a solo hike. It just happened that way, and I was so looking forward to getting on trail that going solo was just fine. Then, the more I thought about it, I realized there was something special about the idea of returning to Zealand Falls, alone. This really fueled the hike's hype. I planned to get to the falls, take a break in the same spot that the Fitchburg State Hiking Club sat on the Bonds Traverse, and get nostalgic. More than a year had passed since the Bonds trip and a lot of peaks were climbed. As I packed the night before, I also made the decision I would swim on this hike. Where? I wasn't exactly sure. Maybe the falls or Zealand Pond. But I packed a small Sea to Summit backpacking towel that I bought at REI from a clearance rack, pretty convinced I was going to use it on this hike.

I parked at the Hale Brook Trailhead (elevation 1,770 feet) along Zealand Road, just 2.5 miles from Route 302. I had a plan to summit Hale quickly, so I could spend time on the back end recreating (swimming, drying, etc.). I had always considered myself a middle-of-the-road hiker in terms of speed. Not fast, not slow. It also never really interested me to move fast. I traditionally hike approximately 2 miles per hour. If the trail is flat and essentially smooth (lacking obstacles such as roots, rocks, etc.), my speed can increase to 3 miles per hour. If ascending or descending elevation, such as climbing up or down mountains, my speed decreases to 1 mile per hour. It's a common and simple formula that I have seen other hikers share. But as noted previously, hikers should always hike their own hike. Meaning, hike at whatever speed suits your body and mind. If somebody you are hiking with tells you otherwise, find a new hiking partner.

The Hale Brook Trail starts with an easy grade but soon becomes moderate. Surprisingly, the first .8 miles climbs nearly 700 feet to 2,460 feet. At the 1.3-mile mark, elevation reaches 3,000 feet. So, while Hale is often considered one of the easier 4,000-footers, the ascent is legit. It's another .9 miles and 1,000 feet to the top. The total vertical gain of 2,300 feet over 2.2 miles supports just how much climbing takes place. I broke a good sweat on the ascension and never really delivered on my plan of summiting fast.

And the summit is viewless. I have read that wasn't always the case but trees have grown, filling in onetime lookouts. There are remains of a fire tower that was removed in 1972. One unique feature of the Hale summit, however, is its magnetic volcanic rocks. Try placing a compass near them and watch the needle dance.

Hale got me to 28/48, but on this day, I was focused on my return to Zealand Falls as well as the Zealand Falls Hut. I made quick work of the summit and soon darted out the Lend-A-Hand Trail after reaching the peak. It was 2.7 miles to the hut and I looked forward to freshening up, checking out the snacks for purchase, and getting some fresh water. I also wanted to get in the falls. There's one lookout along this route but otherwise, it's a keep-on-moving sort of trail. So, I did. I made fast work and got to the hut.

Being a Saturday, in June, it was busy. There were hikers of all ages present, soloists and families. The popular front porch was abuzz, and so were the falls. In hindsight, of course the place was crowded. It's uniquely beautiful and easy to access. However, I was a bit disappointed. I did get a brownie and some lemonade inside. I also had to trek further up the falls than I hoped to carve out a little space to call my own. I did that and reflected upon the Bonds adventure as the water from the falls moved around me. I spent enough time there to get what I needed. Yet, I never really settled in, or relaxed fully. So, I moved on.

I made my way down the Zealand Trail and quickly came upon Zealand Pond. I poked around the shoreline a bit and found a spot that offered just what I was seeking: an area to set up camp and go for a swim. I did just that, and then relaxed, enjoying my lunch along with a cold beverage. The sun was shining and the water was treating me

well, so I stayed a little longer than I expected. I got a few visits and good vibes from passing hikers.

As I stretched out in the water, I felt like all of my hiking experiences had led me to this point. To be alone, in this pond, feeling good, more than halfway through the NH 48 and on schedule to finish on the eve of my 48th birthday. I had 5.1 miles behind me and 3.6 ahead of me, and it was downhill, including a road walk back to the trailhead and my car. I was in a good place and in no rush to go anywhere fast. Then, I felt something odd on my leg under the water. I reached down and kind of rubbed and grabbed my leg. When my hand surfaced, I was holding a leech. It was time to get out of the water.

I toweled off, packed up, and made my way down the Zealand Trail. The stretch from the pond, that first mile or so, delivers stunning views of the surroundings. It was approaching the evening Golden Hour and as I worked my way along the boardwalk that keeps hikers off the marsh and beaver ponds, I kept taking pictures. It was just beautiful. The clouds were reflecting in the ponds. The sun was slowly going down to the west behind the mountains. It was idyllic and I was in the moment, alone.

I think being solo made the difference. I wasn't distracted by trail talk. While I certainly missed my hiking partners, on this day I didn't miss the noise of Hanson's White Mountains history lessons, Engler's high-pitched Ozzy Osbourne lyrics, or Rice's memories of hiking Vermont's Long Trail. All the pieces of my traditional soundtrack were replaced by the subtleties of the area. There were beaver tree corpses littered around the ponds, little fish swimming about, and I was still not fully dried from my swim.

I felt like I was part of the scene as opposed to walking through it. In that moment, I felt part of nature, as corny as it may sound. I believe the swim did that to me, as if I had staked a claim to Zealand Pond. I know I was grateful for the opportunity for things to have worked out as they did. I also know I was careful to not disturb things the best I could, as I believe in Leave No Trace (LNT) or "leave nothing but footprints."

It was a perfect day.

## CLIFF NOTES: WMS CHAPTER 15

🥾 Hiking speed is irrelevant; hike at the speed that suits your body and mind.

🥾 In addition to overnight accommodations, AMC huts offer hikers a chance to use a bathroom, purchase snacks, and fill your water bottles.

🥾 Solo hiking removes the traditional trail-talk soundtrack; you may be surprised how you fill the void.

**Facebook Post:**

Keith Gentili
June 8, 2014

ROAD TO 48 UPDATE (Mt. Hale 4,055)—Snuck in a solo climb yesterday of Mt. Hale and looped in Zealand Hut/Falls/Pond (great family hike). Total hike 8.7 miles, 2,300 feet of elevation gain but all in first 2.2 miles, 6 hours. That's 28 down and 20 remain with 15 months to get it done.

# CHAPTER 16
# The Weatherman Speaks

Date: Thursday, June 12, 2014
Mountain Range: Kinsman
Peak/Elevation (feet): Cannon 4,100
Route (Out and Back): Kinsman Ridge to Rim
Total Distance: 4.4 miles
Hiking Partners: None
Road to 48: #29

In June of 2012, my oldest daughter Julia was finishing fourth grade at New Boston Central School. I was fortunate to chaperone her end-of-the-year class field trip to the White Mountains, and specifically Franconia Notch. The first stop? The Flume Gorge, a great way to spend a few hours. Along with Julia, I had two other students under my supervision and we had a ball touring the place. We took a bunch of silly pictures, played a variety of fun little games, and laughed our way through the attraction's two-mile loop and gift shop.

From there, the buses and parents—traveling separately—went north to Cannon Mountain Ski Resort, where we had lunch and visited the New England Ski Museum. Plus, the entire fourth grade got to ride Cannon's Aerial Tramway 10 minutes to the summit. This was a great thrill for the kids as well as myself. It had been less than a month since my May 18, 2012 hike of the Franconia Ridge Loop (see Chapter 1) and here I was, directly across the street at an elevation of 4,100 feet, with my 10-year-old daughter, staring right at the summit of Mount Lafayette. It was surreal.

As a reminder, during the remainder of my 2012 hiking season, I targeted Franconia Notch peaks exclusively. Flume and Liberty in August. Then the Kinsmans in September, followed by Moosilauke in October. I never climbed Cannon. I also bypassed it during my entire "sophomore" hiking year of 2013. This was not by mistake. Why?

Because I knew my youngest daughter, Sarah, along with her fourth-grade class, would be participating in the Flume/Cannon field trip in 2014 and I would volunteer to chaperone again (I chaperoned every field trip I could for both daughters up through sixth grade; they were always so much fun). Then, at the conclusion of the trip, when the kids boarded the buses in the Cannon parking lot to return to New Boston, I would get on trail and finally finish the NH 48 peaks of Franconia Notch.

This would not be the first time I turned one of my daughter Sarah's school field trips into a peak-bagging adventure. In the fall of 2011, she was in second grade and her class visited the Mt. Kearsarge Indian Museum in Warner. Focusing on Native American culture across North America, it's the only Native museum located in New Hampshire. And it's great. We had a blast traveling back in time and, as a bonus, Rollins State Park and the base of Mount Kearsarge (2,937 feet) was just a few minutes from the parking lot. So, I climbed it. I had to as 3,000-foot mountains in southern New Hampshire are few and deliver great views. Kearsarge is one of those mountains and has a place on another New Hampshire hiking list, the "52 With a View." It is (somewhat) commonly accepted that these two lists, the NH 48 and 52 With a View, feature New Hampshire's 100 best mountains for hikers.

On the morning of Thursday, June 12, 2014, I caught up with Miss Jen's fourth-grade class at the gates of the Flume Gorge. I located my daughter Sarah and began our two-mile loop. Just as it was two years earlier with Julia, it was a hoot. We had fun chasing water and each other. Everything was on schedule as we departed for Cannon. But then the news broke of high winds on the mountain and particularly the summit. As parents began to arrive at the second stop, rumors were spreading that the Aerial Tramway was closed due to the wind. Wind? What wind? It was a relatively nice, calm day here in the parking lot. The students certainly felt that way. These rumors were quickly confirmed.

However, the teachers had a backup plan; a good one. Students and parents were instructed to head for the Old Man of the Mountain Profiler Plaza, which was dedicated exactly three years earlier (June 12, 2011). Located within walking distance of the Cannon parking lot, it served as an ideal conclusion to the day. This attraction celebrates the spirit of the Old Man of the Mountain, New Hampshire's iconic rock formation that collapsed on May 3, 2003. In short, folks stand in a certain spot in the plaza based on their height and they get to see what the Old Man of the Mountain once looked like. It works and is uniquely New Hampshire.

As the New Boston Central School buses were loading fourth graders in the Cannon parking lot, I was loading my backpack. I then walked over and waved goodbye to Sarah as well as my wife Carrie, who was now working at the school as a para-educator, as I could see them both through the bus windows. I turned, and headed for the start of Kinsman Ridge Trail (elevation 1,980 feet). As I walked toward the trailhead, I got it in my head that I needed to find a cool way to help the kids understand that wind conditions on a mountain are much different from wind in a parking lot. After all, the wind significantly altered the course of their day.

In some ways, the Cannon hike already felt like a real victory for me as it was happening on a Thursday, a school day. Plus, I spent much of the day with my wife and daughter. Now, it was early afternoon and I was minutes from a trailhead. This also meant I wasn't spending another weekend day away from my family to hike and that was important to me, especially during these years.

"If you hiked on a Saturday, you would always rally the family to spend Sunday together. I know you always felt hiking made you appreciate your family more. That the time away from us made you enjoy our time together even more," said Carrie. "I don't ever remember you missing anything of significance because you were hiking the 48."

As I was planning the Cannon hike, I did try to flesh out the possibility of Carrie and Sarah joining me. It would not have been the first time a student joined their parent for the return ride home from a field trip as opposed to boarding the bus. It certainly was not encouraged, and Carrie essentially quashed the idea from the beginning. She was not interested in hiking 4,000-foot mountains.

"I do wonder if I had embraced it, if I had tried to join you and climb them as well, how different of an experience it would have been for our family. But I understood where we were as a family and how you were better served to be out there with your hiking partners," she said. "It also encouraged me to embrace the time to explore my own interests. Because you were scheduling your hikes, I knew I would have the day to myself, or with the girls, and could do anything. That was healthy."

The Kinsman Ridge Trail is steep as the summit is just 2.2 miles from the parking but 2,120 feet above it. Plus, the trail is gnarly due to erosion. It's like hiking in a trench. At the same time, rewards can come fast. It's only 1.5 miles to the top of the Cannon Cliffs, which provide outstanding views on a clear day. However, this was not one of them. As I ascended, the trail crossed some backwoods ski areas and the footing seemed to only get worse. I had made pretty quick work of the lower section as I was motivated to get up higher into the wind. But it was slow going up top as things got steeper. I also kept trying to come up with an idea that would somehow tie my hike back to the field trip to connect with the students.

Once I hit the outlook at the cliffs, which is at an elevation of 3,800 feet, I began to get a good idea of just how real the winds were. Visibility was also becoming limited, as weather was worsening. When I was in the parking lot, admittedly, I was curious about the Aerial Tram shutting down and what it took in terms of wind speed to close. However, standing here, still .7 miles from the summit, it made perfect sense. I continued for another .5 miles, where I hit the Rim Trail, 4,000 feet, and heavy fog.

The final .2 miles brought me to the Cannon observation deck. It was totally socked in and there was some precipitation. It wasn't raining, but it was wet. I found a spot that provided some relief from

the wind and sat on the deck. I had a couple of Kind Bars and drank some water. As I was fueling up, it came to me. I could try to film a weather report, local network news style. I was packing my iPhone 4 and, if nothing else, the wind would be certainly apparent. So, I did. While my voice is barely decipherable, the sound of the wind muffling all of the audio is just killer. That, along with the totally gray backdrop and my hair being blown all over the place is pretty convincing that the Aerial Tram should have been shut down. Yep, it was real windy. The folks in charge made the right call, of course.

My return hike was slow. The trench was significantly more difficult to navigate going down than up. The footing was worse and it just made for a cautious slog. However, at 2.2 miles in distance, that was fine. I got back down to the car safely, updated the family, and made my way home. I also sent Carrie the video I shot on the summit. I asked her to play it for her class the next day and she did.

That made me happy. I felt that the 28-second video connected me back to the students and the field trip. Conversely, I felt it connected the students to the top of Cannon. After all, they were supposed to summit the mountain that day. And now, thanks to my little 4.4-mile hike, the students did get to see the summit and what the weather not only looked like, but sounded like. It was a little thing, but it made me proud to be a hiker.

**Facebook Post:**

Keith Gentili
June 12, 2014

NOT-SO-FISHY—Well, after the school buses left Cannon, I went on a little mission to get answers. Two hours, 2.2 miles, and 2,300 feet of elevation gain later, bagged NH 4000-footer peak No. 29 and got to the bottom of this "high winds" hoopla.

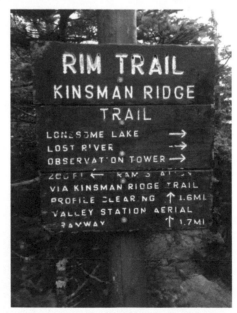

# CHAPTER 17
# 12 Miles in 12 Hours

Date: Saturday, August 9, 2014
Mountain Range: Presidential
Peak/Elevation (feet): Adams 5,799, Madison 5,366
Route (Loop): Air Line to Short Line to King Ravine to Subway to
 King Ravine to Gulf Side to Air Line to Star Lake to Osgood to
 Air Line
Total Distance: 12 miles
Hiking Partners: Eric Hanson, Eric Engler, Keith Rice
Road to 48: #30, #31

Throughout the summer of 2014, I was working on a plan to summit Mount Adams and Mount Madison that would include hiking through King Ravine. The more I read about going across, over, and under its Subway and boulder field as well as visiting its ice caves, the more King Ravine fascinated me. I also knew going straight up the headwall at its south end on the ascent to Adams, one of the steepest climbs in the White Mountains, was a must. All of the photos I had seen from this spot were just too perfect to even consider an alternate plan. King Ravine not only matched the approach established at the outset of the NH 48, it best embodied it. This would be the next hike, but because of the challenge it posed in climbing two of the state's biggest mountains, I wanted to be sure I had support.

The plan went out to Hanson, Engler, and Rice without a date. I told them it was going to be big hike and I thought it would be best if we could all make it. I believe, on some level, there is strength in numbers. This certainly was the case for the four of us on trail as we often paired up when we separated. After some discussion and fleshing out of the calendar, we were able to find a date that worked for all of us, August 9.

It's worth noting that, after hiking twice in June (Hale and Cannon), I did not summit an NH 48 peak in July of 2014. My wife Carrie had an emergency appendectomy early that month and her recovery was derailed by an infection. We were fortunate to have a visiting nurse come to our home each day to check on her progress as well as change her bandages. However, the infection continued throughout the summer and Carrie made a few return trips to the hospital. Needless to say, hiking was not a priority during this time.

As the Adams/Madison date crept closer, discussions shifted to execution. It became apparent that the size and scope of this hike, 10-plus miles with 5,000 feet of elevation gain, lent itself to be part of an overnight trip. After a few ideas were tossed aside, Hanson suggested the winning entry. His younger brother Craig, along with his buddies, had an annual Tripoli Road camping trip in early August. It just so happened that this year, they would be at the site the weekend of August 9 and had room for the four of us. Plus, there was plenty of parking along Tripoli Road and it would serve as the ideal meet spot.

"My brother's camping trip worked out perfectly for us. I went up there the night before the hike. But the night before that, Elsa flipped over in the crib for the first time and she kept flipping over and over. I was going on no sleep and was running on fumes that whole weekend," said Hanson. "You guys met me on Tripoli Road at my brother's camp that morning and we all drove to the trailhead in Engler's car. I remember hearing Widespread Panic's cover of the Talking Heads song 'Heaven' as we were approaching Appalachia [trailhead]. Between the view of the mountains and it being a beautiful sunny morning, I remember thinking, this is so great."

"That was my 1997 Lincoln Town Car," said Engler. "It had a 10-CD changer in the trunk, but that was definitely not my CD."

It was mine. I had discovered Widespread Panic in the summer of 1992 and have stayed with them to this day. "Heaven" is the final track on the band's 1988 debut album "Space Wrangler." After Jerry Garcia's death in 1995, I began seeing them more and more. I remember thinking it was odd when my Widespread Panic concert total surpassed the Grateful Dead.

On March 2, 2020, just before COVID shut down much of the Northeast including New Hampshire, I took my daughter Julia to see Widespread Panic at the Beacon Theatre in New York City. It was my 40th time seeing them, her first. While the band did not play "Heaven" that night, it did deliver a double encore of Talking Heads songs ("City of Dreams" and "Life During Wartime") as a tribute to the New York City/CBGB legends. Julia's takeaway as the house lights came up, "Dad, it was fun seeing you dance and be so happy." For the record, I have also seen (at her request) Demi Lovato, One Direction, and a Harry Styles solo concert with her and enjoyed them all.

When we arrived at Appalachia that morning in Randolph, we had to park along Route 2, about a quarter-mile west of the trailhead. The combination of Rice, Engler, and I all traveling individually from our homes to Hanson's brother's camp, and then transferring our gear into Engler's car, resulted in a late start (11am). But we were here now, and knowing we only had an hour drive back to Tripoli Road after the hike was comforting. We got on trail.

The network of trails from the Appalachia trailhead (elevation 1,306 feet) is a never-ending, crisscrossing forested labyrinth. There are trails running north-south, east-west, and every other direction. It really is a maze, but the signs are good and we had maps. Plus, our plan was simple; take the Air Line Trail to the Short Line Trail, and that gets us to the Subway, boulder field, and ice caves. So, we did just that and reached the junction of the King Ravine Trail at 2.7 miles (3,150 feet). Here we got a taste of the boulders and continued to climb. It felt like being on the set of *Jurassic Park*, as if a pair of Velociraptors were suddenly going to appear from behind the giant rocks. We reached the Subway 3.2 miles from the trailhead at an elevation of 3,775.

"That was a fun stretch," said Rice. "Down and around the boulders and there was still ice in August."

It was fun, and completely unique. I had built the ascent of this hike around the Subway, and the boulders, so it was nice to see it live up to our expectations. We got our big adventure all through this area.

"We were scooting under stuff, squeezing through the holes, and going over boulders," said Hanson. "It was cool but it took a lot of gas out of us as we were monkeying around in there for a bit."

Well, three of us were. Engler, who often beats to his own drum, elected to bypass this route.

"There was no way I was going through the boulder field," said Engler. "That's just not how I hike. I'm taking the direct route up. My body was already stressed."

The direct route up did include going straight up the headwall at the end of King Ravine. Just how steep would this climb be? According to *The 4000-Footers of the White Mountains*, the headwall starts at the 3.5-mile mark (4,000 feet) and climbs 1,100 feet in .5 miles. As I noted in a previous chapter, gaining 100 feet of elevation every .1 mile is steep. Your body will feel that and when climbing NH 48 peaks, at some point that type of gain traditionally occurs. However, this was going to be more than double that, an average of 220 feet per .1 mile.

"The headwall was straight up. Just awesome," said Hanson. "It was worth turning around and checking how great the view was every 10 feet we climbed."

After being separated through some of the boulder field, the Fitchburg State Hiking Club reassembled to take on the King Ravine headwall as a group. We worked our way up methodically, stopping to enjoy the view and fueling up as we went. We were staying hydrated and eating snacks. While there was some pre-hike concern about its steepness, we navigated the headwall cleanly.

"I felt we went right up King Ravine. I don't recall any trouble getting up the headwall," said Rice. "We did all right. We got up to the junction and made our way up to Adams."

Engler's perspective of his hiking ability was evolving during this time. He repeatedly shared his feelings on being inexperienced during previous hikes and what that meant for him. Looking back on this trip, he noted a sense of confidence was starting to develop.

"In between the Cabot Hike [Chapter 13] and this one, I did the Osceolas with my son, Zach. Adams and Madison would be my 17th and 18th 4,000-footers. I still had the same mentality in preparation. I'd log on to the common websites and take a brief look at the trails that we were going to do. I always had a narrow view of our plans though as hiking the 48 was never my goal," he said. "But now I started to think, this is something I could do. I had hiked in winter; I got through the challenges of King Ravine and did the Osceolas with my son. I was gaining confidence. I was okay with some of these hikes now."

From the top of the headwall, we had less than a mile to the summit of Adams (5,799 feet), New Hampshire's second highest mountain. This area is pure rock, including a scattering of big slabs of granite, and we made our way to the peak by rock hopping. There were a few other folks on Adams, including a group of summit squatters.

"Summit squatters," said Rice. "They're horrible."

So, we found a spot on the southeast corner of Adams and soaked up, arguably, one of the best views in the White Mountains. We were staring straight down into the Great Gulf Wilderness and all its glory. The Jefferson Ravine was right below our feet and the summit of El Jefe seemed like it was in our kitchen. We also had the quintessential look at Mount Washington including much of the auto road. To call it a postcard would be underselling it. I felt we were on top of the world, or at the least, on top of New Hampshire.

"That spot was money," said Hanson. "One of my favorite spots in the Whites. That view is unbelievable."

We remained on the top of Adams for more than an hour. We ate lunch and celebrated our climb with a summit toast. Everything was on track as we discussed our next move, which was to go down the backside of Adams via the seldom-used Star Lake Trail. This was the second part of getting the most bang for our buck. The Star Lake Trail is steep but it helped make our route a loop hike. Plus, there were some unique features on that side of the mountain worth seeing, including Star Lake and large outcroppings of white quartz. But then we were thrown a curve.

"The cap on one of the Jim Beam plastic bottles broke during lunch. That's why I had to carry it down the Star Lake Trail," said Hanson.

Admittedly, as a group we enjoyed our experiences on each summit. They represented the reward for getting up the mountain. But we were generally reserved, especially when other hikers were present. If we were alone on a peak, which was often the case, yes, we might dial it up. But the idea that Hanson was going to carry a plastic Jim Beam bottle in his hand while descending Adams didn't really sit well with me. I just didn't like the idea of drawing that kind of attention.

"I couldn't put in my pack," said Hanson, of the 750-milliliter bottle called the Traveler. "To this day, I still don't know how it got smashed. Somebody must have stepped on it."

There was a moment when the four of us were working our way

down the Star Lake Trail and we thought we would be better served to just drink it. We were essentially alone on the trail but would soon be nearing the Madison Hut, where we would see a good amount of hiker traffic. That was our brilliant solution to solving the problem of having to carry it.

"We were hitting it a bit on the way down," said Engler. "We were trying."

Alas, it wasn't to be. We reached the point of diminishing returns. Meaning, we still had a big climb ahead in Madison, the state's fifth biggest mountain (named for our fourth president) and a long hike back out to the car. Emptying a bottle of 80-proof bourbon was not our best play. Rather, we made our way past the hut in a somewhat stealth manner and took on our final ascent of the day.

"That last push up Madison, I was exhausted," said Hanson. "And I was still hiking with a plastic bottle in my hand. But I hid it as we went past the hut."

We reached the summit of Madison (5,366 feet), and while tired, we knew it was all downhill from here. We had hiked 6.1 miles to this point, worked our way through the boulder field/Subway, climbed a headwall, and two big peaks. We knew we had about 4.5 miles back to the car. I wanted to take the Air Line Trail back along the Durand Ridge. This would take us right along the edge of King Ravine and allow us to look down into our midday playground. This would also complete our loop and everyone was on board. We would relax for a while on Madison and then start the final leg of the hike.

"You had saved a round of beers for Madison," Hanson recalled. "We each had one and were toasting our summit, and I dropped mine. It fell on a rock and spilled and you were mad. You, Engler, and I were distracted by that while Riceman was trying to get our attention."

Added Engler, "I remember Rice was mouthing words to me, but I couldn't understand him."

Said Rice, "The way we were sitting, we all had our own space. Madison is a true cone of a summit, a pyramid. From where I was, I could see over an edge and I could see a couple right below the peak. She was flashing him and he was taking pictures. I turned around and was trying to get your attention. I was going, 'You guys. You guys.' I got the full view. It was a gutsy play by her as they were on the approach side from the hut. It was probably for some Instagram-challenge thing."

Admittedly, I missed the show as I was caught up in Hanson dropping the 16-ounce, high-end IPA I just carried more than six miles. But he confirmed the incident.

"Rice was saying, 'Guys. Hey guys.' And when we resurfaced from saving my beer," said Hanson, "Rice was like, 'You guys missed it. The girl was topless, and her boyfriend was taking photos.' And we didn't believe him at first. We missed it because we were squabbling over my spilt beer."

"It really was a guy taking pictures of his girlfriend with her top off," said Engler. "Then they left and Rice was like, 'Noooo'."

"I will also say they were guilty of too much PDA," said Hanson. "And I got a creepy vibe from the boyfriend. Plus, they were total summit hogs. They sat on the summit for a long time. We waited a while before we got the summit."

130

As we worked our way down Madison, we could feel Golden Hour oozing in. It was a gorgeous summer evening and we made our way over to the Air Line Trail. It added a little distance to our hike but this provided us the walk along the edge of King Ravine I wanted. It was during the next few miles that the Fitchburg State Hiking Club was "hitting the note" once again. The upper section of the Air Line Trail gave us spectacular 360 views. To our left and down was King Ravine. To our right and up was Madison. Adams was just right behind us.

"The view was awesome, the sun was setting," said Hanson. "We took some great photos."

"It really was beautiful that day," said Engler.

At one point, an ascending solo hiker stopped to talk to us for a bit. After a pleasant conversation about the day's events, he took our picture and it really captures our group during the height of our NH 48.

"I have that photo framed in my office," said Hanson.

The challenge, however, of the upper Air Line Trail was we were now boulder hopping again and that made for slow going, as fatigue was setting in for all of us. Yes, we were having fun but we still had about three miles to get back to Appalachia when we finally reached treeline. It was here we agreed it was time to put a push on our return.

Or at least try to make our way out efficiently.

"From there it just started getting dark," said Hanson. "And we were tired, and we all ended up off trail."

As was often the case, we did separate into pairs. Rice and I became the front group. We were making decent time but as the ground began to flatten out, we both realized we got caught up in the labyrinth and got off the trail. As hard as we tried to find our way back to Air Line, we couldn't.

"That was a long walk out. There's a huge network of trails there and it's easy to get lost and we did," said Rice. "We had to hoof it back to the car."

The nice thing about that area is that, eventually, traffic can be heard on Route 2, especially the trucks. So, as long as you keep moving north, you will run into the road. When we reached Route 2, we were maybe a half-mile west of the trailhead and that put us maybe a quarter of a mile from the car. Hanson and Engler were not as fortunate.

"Hanson and I walked down the last few miles together. It got dark and we lost the trail," said Engler. "We came down into a field, we could see fence posts and just didn't know where we were. We ended up being way to the left, west, of the trailhead [Appalachia]. When we hit Route 2, we realized just how far off we were. I called Rice and asked him to drive my car down to us. He said, 'No.' In the end, we might have been a full mile down. That asshole. Ha."

Rice and I were sitting on Engler's trunk when the call came. Thanks to the 1997 Lincoln Town Car's fancy coded power locks (Engler gave us the code), we had access to the vehicle and were able to get comfortable waiting. As we sat there, we did some math. Adding for the extra distance due to our error, we realized that we had hiked 12 miles and were on trail for 12 hours as it was now 11pm. It became our catch phrase for the rest of the night.

"It was a big boy hike; 12 miles in 12 hours. We turned it into a great loop," said Rice. "And we did spend a good amount of time on top of both peaks."

We continued to wait for Engler and Hanson. In the end, we just didn't realize how far west they must have drifted. It took a while before Engler arrived, and he arrived alone.

"I was mad that I had to walk back along Route 2," said Engler. "I had given you guys the code to my car. You had access to the key. I was exhausted and aggravated that Rice wouldn't drive down to get us. It was a nice night, though."

Added Rice, "Then, we had to go and get Hanson."

So, we did. We loaded up and drove west. We found him still horizontal, lying on the edge of Route 2's pavement, sort of in the bike lane. He climbed into the car.

"For me, that was my first hike where my body really did run out of gas for real," said Hanson. "I was taking it 10 yards at a time at the end. I just hadn't slept in a few nights, and the 12 miles and 5,000 feet of elevation wiped me out. That is why when I reached Route 2, I just laid down and told Engler to pick me up where I was. I slept the whole way back to Tripoli Road."

We got back to Craig Hanson's camp and received a bit of a hero's welcome. We had been gone 14 hours; we departed from there around 10am and now it was midnight. The gang was happy to see to us.

"They had a huge fire going and fed us," said Rice.

"I had my generator in my car along with my blender. I made a round of frozen mudslides. One of Craig's buddies said I could come back any time because nobody had ever made them mudslides at the site before," said Engler. "The next day, my wife and kids were camping on a river in the area and I met them. At one point, I was swimming with my family. I looked down and noticed my ankles were the fattest they ever were in my life. Just swollen. They were huge. I couldn't bend my feet."

## CLIFF NOTES: WMS CHAPTER 17

🏃 Be watchful of all trail markers or confusing cross trails as it can turn a 10-mile hike into a 12-mile hike.

🏃 Never squabble over spilt beer. You may just miss something.

🏃 Be courteous to your fellow hikers; don't be a summit squatter.

🏃 It's okay to both embrace solo hiking and cherish your hiking partners.

🏃 Eat well on trail especially if it makes you happy, as a great meal can really make a difference.

🏃 Try to get that one special photo on each adventure that says it all.

---

**Facebook Post:**

Keith Gentili
August 12, 2014

ROAD TO 48 UPDATE: MT. ADAMS (5,799) & MT. MADISON (5,366)—After taking July off, got back out there Saturday for a long one; 12 miles, 12 hours, and 5,000 feet of vertical while knocking off NH's No. 2 & No. 5 highest peaks. Key piece of this one: King Ravine Trail and taking on its caves and headwall; 31 down, 17 to go.

# CHAPTER 18
# Bucket the Hiking Guide

Date: Friday-Saturday, September 5-6, 2014
Mountain Range: Carter-Moriah
Peak/Elevation (feet): Wildcat D 4,062, Wildcat 4,422, Carter
  Dome 4,832, South Carter 4,430, Middle Carter 4,610
Route (Thru Hike): Wildcat Ridge to Carter-Moriah to North
  Carter to Imp
Total Distance: 14.8 miles
Hiking Partners to Carter Notch Hut: Ron Reimer, Jason Unger,
  Jamie Neefe, Len Wolfe
Hiking Partners from Carter Notch Hut: None
Road to 48: #32, #33, #34, #35, #36

Throughout my adult life, I have been fortunate to have many friendships mature and evolve as I've aged. This is true with a good number of folks from both college and high school. Like many people, I've also developed some very strong relationships through work. In fact, at each stop in my career, I always seemed to connect with at least one individual thanks to a common interest in music or sports or craft beer. It has kind of happened organically for me, and while my record is far from perfect, this approach has served my life and my family well.

Until I reached New Boston. My wife and I bought our house in 2001. I made the decision to not actively seek new friends in town. With two kids in diapers, a mortgage, and a career that included a significant amount of business travel, I felt my plate was full. In 2009, Carrie claimed a free swing set from the bulletin board at the daycare center where she was working. It was the big wooden kind, complete with a tower featuring a slide and fort. Our daughters were now of the age where they repeatedly asked for a swing set, so it was the right move. I rented a U-Haul, drove to the house giving it away, and got to work disassembling it. Alone. Things went slow. Real slow. It became a two-day job. Eventually, it was time to load the tower onto the U-Haul. I just couldn't maneuver it solo. It was too big and too heavy.

The realization that I really didn't have anyone local to call for help was tough to swallow. Except, I knew that I had made this decision years earlier. This was my fault and the result of it, well, made me sad.

Then a neighbor, not my neighbor but a resident on the street with the swing set, showed up. He had seen me struggling from his driveway. We got the tower loaded and I was on my way. That swing set still sits on my property today and my daughters still use it from time to time. That makes me happy.

In February of 2014, I was invited to play darts at a house in town. I went. I met some folks, had fun, and was invited back. This cycle repeated itself a few times during the month and I quickly found myself part of a group I would begin referring to as the New Boston Dads. We all had daughters in the same Girl Scout Troop and we all really enjoyed each other's company. These nights were filled with good talk, good music (on vinyl), good beer, and a lot of fun.

By the time March rolled around, I had spoken of my pursuit of the New Hampshire 48 on a few occasions. My hiking season was about to begin, so I put out feelers. I told the New Boston Dads my plan was to hike once a month throughout 2014 and there was an open invitation. And while nobody jumped on that idea, I also suggested planning a weekend backpacking trip specifically for the group. Ron Reimer and Jason Unger were immediately interested.

"We knew you were hiking a lot. I was always interested in bigger hikes but I was apprehensive of them. And I'd never backpacked," said Reimer. "You threw the idea out there. Jake and I both gravitated toward it quickly. You threw out options: the Bonds, the Southern Presidentials, the Northern Presidentials. But the main focus was the Wildcats-Carters-Moriah Traverse."

It didn't take long for the idea to become a thing. So much so that by mid-March, we officially locked in the date for a Wildcats-Carters-Moriah Traverse. Here's the email I sent Reimer and Unger on March 16 confirming the plan for the weekend following Labor Day, September 5-7, 2014.

*From: Keith Gentili*

*Subject: Wildcats-Carters-Moriah Hike: Sept 5-7*

*Date: March 16, 2014 at 6:40:27 PM EDT*

*To: Jason Unger, Ron Reimer*

*Okay, very cool. Glad you guys like the plan.*

*Now we can keep nailing down specific roles, needs, etc. based on our own expertise such as music, fire, and meals (breakfast vs lunch vs dinner).*

*Also, I will hike at least one day a month April to Oct., so we can do a day trip together. This summer I'm hitting the presidentials, so lots of great stuff to choose from. Last summer was Sandwich Range and 2012 was Franconia Notch.*

Throughout the spring and summer of 2014, the New Boston Dads continued to get together regularly. There was more good talk, good music, and good beer. There was also more good planning for the September 5-7 Wildcats-Carters-Moriah Traverse. Not only was I getting excited about the trip, everyone else was really engaged in the preparations. Each time we assembled, when the discussion shifted to the trip, it was always lively, animated, and articulate.

However, nobody else was hiking. Ever. Despite my constant encouragement, whenever I would ask, "Did anyone get on trail over the weekend?" I would get a full round of "Nopes." As the summer progressed, and days got a little shorter, this became more and more concerning. I knew the trip called for big miles and vertical gain, especially the first day. Yet, these guys were still all in and the weekend itinerary continued to come together.

"I was telling a co-worker about our plan," said Reimer. "He offered us his cabin for the night before the hike. I had stayed at his place before with my family. It's in Intervale, which is right down the road from the Wildcats trailhead. So, I secured it. He even suggested that we walk from his cabin to the Tuckerman Tavern for dinner."

September 1 arrived, and while the New Boston Dads had still not been on a hike that season, I had grown tremendously fond of each of them during this time. It was genuine affection based on our seven months of regularly getting together. Plus, I really believed we had a great weekend backpacking trip planned, which now included Thursday night in a cabin followed by two nights in shelters, 20 miles on trail, and summiting six official 4,000-footers. This was shaping up to be a monster adventure.

However, there was one asterisk that, for me, put the whole trip in jeopardy. Carrie was still dealing with the infection from her emergency appendectomy back in July. It just wouldn't go away. And with the school year now starting, she was returning to work and that meant she could no longer receive visiting-nurse services. In short, it was my turn to carry the heavy lifting in terms of changing her bandages each day. Thus, three nights away for backpacking was not a guarantee. Nevertheless, as the driving force of this trip, I felt it was my duty to keep things on track. We had been working on it for six months, and until the Mrs. shut it down officially, I had to continue to lead. Thus, here was my email on September 1 to Reimer and Unger laying out the agenda.

*From: Keith Gentili*

*Subject: RE: Wildcats-Carters-Moriah Hike: Sept 5-7*

*Date: On September 1, 2014 12:17 PM EDT*

*To: Jason Unger, Ron Reimer*

*I'll apologize up front if I'm throwing too much at you but here's a reminder of the 4 legs:*

*DAY 1*

*A) Rt. 16/Glen Ellis Falls parking to Carter Notch: 5 miles with all 5 Wildcat Peaks*

*B) Carter Notch to Imp Shelter: 7.5 miles with 5 peaks (the Carters, Hight, and Zeta Pass)*

*DAY 2*

*C) Imp Shelter to Rattle River Shelter: 6.1 miles with Moriah and 8.7 if we add Shelburne Moriah.*

*DAY 3*

*D) Rattle River Shelter to Rt. 2: 1.7 miles.*

*Few other quick tips:*

*a) Cut your toenails short prior to Thursday...it makes a difference.*

*b) Bring a bandana if you got one; many uses.*

*c) If you really like flavor/spices with food; bring some (oregano, parsley, garlic powder, tabasco, olive oil, etc.), no added weight but can add taste.*

*d) Ziploc bags are your friends...no weight and can hold anything.*

*e) Gloves/beanie/extra wool socks always key.*

*f) Friday weather looks outstanding; Saturday 50% chance rain...so be prepared with hood/rain hat, etc.*

*g) Gaiters (tall or short) will help keep boots dry in rain/snow if you have them or considering a gear run.*

*Also, thinking about lunch at Carter Notch as opposed to Mt. Hight...fuel up sooner for 2nd Leg of Day 1.*

*Last, I will not be bringing beer due to weight (sausages and chicken salad are a bit heavy), I look forward to helping others lighten their load of beer if necessary...think 1 lb. per can.*

*Here's my official booze bring:*

*750 of Vodka for Hard Arnold Palmers at shelter as I'll have lemonades/ iced tea, etc.*

*750 of Jim Beam for drinks at shelter.*

*16 ounces of Baileys for morning coffee, I have coffee singles.*

*Gear reminder, I'll have:*

*Stove/propane/pots*

*Water filter*

*Fire starters*

*Tarp (6x8)*

*Bug spray*

*Moleskin for blisters*

*Minor first aid kit*

*Extra headlamp to light shelter*

*Advil/Alleve*

*Map*

*Trail guide*

As the countdown to the trip reached its final days, it became apparent I couldn't take three nights off from my family responsibilities. My solution was to hike out on Saturday, after summiting Mount Moriah, the trip's final 4,000-footer. The group could then continue to Rattle River Shelter without me. The good news was the trip was on. I'd be getting the six NH 48 peaks I needed as well as two nights away. This was a huge win. Everyone was excited and we got out of town quickly on Thursday, September 4, after work. We were headed straight to the cabin to get organized. Then, we would take Reimer's co-worker's advice and walk to the Tuckerman Tavern for some eats and drinks.

"Before we got to the tavern, we spotted a car at the Rattle River parking area," said Reimer. "I got a picture of the Appalachian Trail sign that night knowing it was the end of our hike. Spotting a car, that was a brand-new idea to me."

We enjoyed some wings and beers at the tavern before walking home. We had plenty of hike prep to get to including preparing our packs, as well as inventorying gear and food. I volunteered to make the next day's meals, so I par-boiled a bunch of sausages and caramelized some onions and peppers. Of course, we were also getting caught up in the moment and that meant enjoying a few beverages. I remember being on the front porch pretty late in the evening, music playing, and Reimer cracking a fresh beer with a smile. It was midnight. I asked him what he opened.

"It was a Ten FIDY," said Reimer, of the Oskar Blues Imperial Stout that gets its name from its alcohol content, 10.5% ABV.

This was a sign. We needed to be on trail as early as possible in the morning and still had another car (mine) to spot. We made the decision to move it inside and shut it down after Reimer's Ten FIDY was gone. We had six months' planning into the trip, and here it was. Day 1 loomed with a big climb and 12 miles from the parking lot to the Imp Shelter, our destination. We needed to get some sleep.

"You guys drank pretty hard. I was nervous for the hike so I didn't," said Jamie Neefe. "I was worried about my knees crapping out and me being the weak link."

Friday morning came fast but we got moving early. The fact that we were just 20 minutes from the trailhead was a savior. We dropped my car at the Carter-Moriah Trailhead, where I planned to be exiting Saturday afternoon after hiking about 6.5 miles on the second day. We then returned to the Glen Ellis Falls parking area (elevation 1,960 feet), which sits directly across the street from the start of the Wildcat Ridge Trail.

"We were in the parking lot and I remember looking across the street and wondering where we were going to hike," said Neefe. "It

140

couldn't be up the face of what we were looking at. Who would put a trail there?"

Reimer took a picture of Unger and me at 8:01am just as we crossed under Route 16, packs on and smiling. The Ellis River water crossing was our next step. We looked good. But...

"It was a shit show," said Reimer. "A minute into the hike, we lost Neefe. He was gone and I fell into the river; both of my feet went in."

It's true. My career as a hiking guide was less than five minutes old and I had already lost a member of our group, while another just soaked his boots and socks with 12 miles ahead of us. We did find our missing hiking partner. Neefe had taken a right toward Glen Ellis Falls. He was now back with the group.

"I guess I was first, because I got under the road and followed the trail to the right. After five minutes of not seeing anyone, I wandered back to see what you idiots were doing," said Neefe. "Who was the real idiot?"

Yep, it was bad, but things could only go up from here...and that happened to be where the trail was headed.

"Straight up and hilarious," said Reimer. "At 8:23am, Neefe and Wolfe were sitting down and dazed. We were on trail for all of 20 minutes."

The Wildcat Ridge Trail ascends from Route 16 in Pinkham Notch as steep as any trail in the Whites. The first .9 miles climbs nearly 1,100 feet. The next .6 miles gains another 700 feet. And while there is some infrastructure to help, including rock stairs, wooden steps, and a ladder, it's so rugged and taxing that it's impossible to enjoy. Even the views, outstanding during this stretch, are difficult to appreciate.

"It's known as one of the toughest sections of the Whites," said Reimer.

Thanks to two days of supplies and a group with limited (or no) experience, we were all carrying heavy packs. And with absolutely no warm-up mileage to find our stride and ease into the hike, this adventure was starting to derail.

"You were our fearless leader, full of energy and positivity. The rest of us not so much," said Neefe. "You were singing songs to try to keep us engaged as our heart rates quickly raced to 120 beats per minute. After a quarter of a mile, I was thinking to myself, 'This is a mistake. You have 11.75 miles to go,' and panic set in."

In hindsight, we should have shut it down earlier the night before. But as we all know, hindsight is 20-20, and, well, we were having way too much fun to even consider that in real time. But during our first 1.5 miles we climbed 1,800 feet, and that took the wind out of the group. I felt if we could just get to the Wildcat ski gondolas, essentially the two-mile mark, we would achieve our first peak, rest, and regroup.

"I was puking before we reached the ski area. I was a mess," Reimer told me. "But you saw me melting down and told me I'd be okay. You tried to keep me preoccupied. You could see the disaster starting to form and you started making a bunch small talk about music and song lyrics, and then we sang a bunch of Steve Miller songs. So that was you just trying to get us guys to the first peak."

"Fly Like an Eagle." "The Joker." "Jet Airliner." Reimer and I banged out a bunch of lyrics before reaching Wildcat E (4,046 feet). I just tried to get him to focus on anything but his hangover. I had hiked hungover plenty of times and knew his pain. I really felt like if I could get him on the other side of it, he'd be fine.

"But then Neefe broke a pole," Unger reminded me. "And you fell to the back of the pack for a while to counsel him in an effort to get him to the first summit. He was a mess. He had aluminum ski poles that bent and snapped."

"I broke my pole coming off a boulder," said Neefe. "It snapped right in half."

Despite these challenges, we made it to the top of the ski area. We removed our packs and dropped them together forming a pile. I felt a sense of victory and expected others to do the same. But that wasn't the case. At one point, a couple Appalachian Trail (AT) thru-hikers—folks making their way from Springer Mountain, Georgia, to Maine's Katahdin—walked by and one commented on both the newness and large size of our individual packs. Not a good sign. Morale was low.

"Part of our planning was us texting each other our pack weights," said Reimer. "I stepped on and off the scale a bunch of times. You said we needed to get down to like 30 pounds and I was over 50 pounds. There was just no way. I had a two-week supply of Clif Bars."

"That was my first time with a full pack and I was shocked at how heavy it was," said Neefe.

My pack, too, was more than 50 pounds. I had never carried this much weight. I was carrying two meals for a party of five, plus a good amount of gear with the group in mind. On the steepest part of the Wildcat ascent, I felt a tweak in my right hip I had never felt before. But I wasn't going to share my struggles as I was trying to help lift the spirits of the others.

Just past the ski area, there's an observation platform signaling the summit of Wildcat D (4,062 feet) and our hike's first official 4,000-footer. We got up on it to enjoy the view. A few older hikers soon arrived, and they, too, commented on our group's packs. I had climbed 31 peaks of the NH 48 and nobody had ever commented on my pack. This was the second mention in less than an hour. Another bad sign.

"The platform on Wildcat D," said Reimer. "The guys asked us how far we were going with those big packs. We told them the Imp Shelter and one said, 'You're really hiking that far?' They made a gentle suggestion, indicating it was going to be more challenging than we thought."

We were now two miles and three hours into a 12-mile hike. I originally believed we could do the 12 miles in 10 hours or so, which would have put us at the Imp Shelter between 6 and 7pm (great). I figured that even if we averaged 1 mph, we would get there at 8pm just as it got really dark (fine). Our next three miles were essentially flat and downhill, it was time to get the group moving. But my enthusiasm was not being met well as the New Boston Dads were

144

shot. Reimer detailed his challenges.

"It was my first time carrying a pack. Plus, I was only two miles into my boots as they were brand new. The alcohol didn't help," he said. "But the biggest thing, in all seriousness, I now know I was dehydrated. Looking back, I hadn't drunk any water the day before and I didn't drink enough on the hike. I was dehydrated."

As we were working our way across the top of the Wildcat Ridge Trail, on a flat section, Wolfe made the announcement he was done. It was apparent others felt the same. It wasn't even noon. Six months planning, and the whole trip blew up in less than four hours, three miles, and one climb. Yet, I knew it was true. I also knew they all had good intentions.

"Although I was relieved when we got up to the relative flatness of the ridge, I was quietly talking to Wolfe," said Neefe. "There was no way I could do this for another nine miles."

They just hadn't put in the miles on trail in preparation. I had seen the Fitchburg State Hiking Club—Hanson, Rice, and Engler—push through these challenges on multiple occasions. I believed this group would too. But that didn't happen. We were two miles away from the Carter Notch Hut and the new plan was to get there, eat lunch, and evaluate.

"I wasn't feeling good that first day either," said Unger. "I was hungover but not as bad as others."

We soon reached the summit of our second official 4,000-footer, Wildcat (4,422 feet), 4.2 miles from the parking lot. Yet, there wasn't much celebrating. We then had a .9-mile descent straight down to the Carter Notch Hut. From the overlook, we could see the hut below.

"Seeing the valley open up and the hut so far below, Wolfe and I both declared that we didn't care what others did, but we were not hiking past that hut," admitted Neefe.

"I don't remember talking about or thinking we were going to stay at the hut," said Reimer. "I do remember looking down on it from there and thinking you gotta be kidding me, we are going down there? That is nuts."

The trail dropped more than 1,000 feet. On the climb down, my right hip was acting up again. I was concerned about it, but I didn't say anything. As a group, we were already limping into the hut and sort of into the unknown. When we arrived, just after 2pm, the group sought out the caretaker. I went straight to the larger of the two Carter Lakes, ponds adjacent to the hut, and went for a swim. It was a hot afternoon on a couple of levels. I needed to cool off. I got what I needed, and so did the others.

"We found out that we could stay at the hut for $125 each. Are you kidding me? Here's my card," said Reimer. "It was money well spent. There was no way I was going to continue on."

Added Unger, "The credit cards came out real fast. It wasn't a question."

"I remember you going for a swim in the small lake as the rest of us were zombified and gladly paying $125 for the night," Neefe recalled.

By the time the group had finalized its hut arrangements, I had finished my swim and began making lunch. I put out a round of chicken-salad wraps featuring some ham slices along with some Cape Cod Chips (single sacks) on the side. We ate lunch and had a beer. Any tension that had formed on the Wildcat Ridge was now gone. The four of them had their overnight accommodations; I had a 1,400-foot climb up to Carter Dome. I bid adieu to the New Boston Dads.

"You made us chicken salad sandwiches. We ate. Then you were gone," said Reimer. "We were trying to see you as you climbed Carter Dome."

I had to press on for a variety of reasons, the largest being my wife. I promised her I'd be home the following day and I was keeping that promise. I had also hardwired myself to bag NH 48 peaks when you could. This was one of those times. Carter Dome would be #34, and I planned to keep on rolling north to South Carter and Middle Carter before I slept. I was worried about the New Boston Dads and how this trip might affect our dynamic. I had grown close to each of them, and as I made my way up Carter Dome, I wasn't sure if I was the bad guy for mapping out this trip.

The 1.2-mile ascent from Carter Notch to Carter Dome is serious, as the vertical gain is more than 100 feet every tenth of a mile. It was still a very hot day, and I was still carrying a heavy load. As I slogged my way up, I often popped out at lookouts and could see my hiking partners below. They were hanging around the pond, relaxing, and likely enjoying another beer. When I reached the Carter

Dome summit (4,832 feet), I was thrilled my climb was over but I was nearly overheating. I took a red-faced selfie in which veins seem to be popping out of my forehead.

From here I made my way .8 miles north to Mount Hight (4,675 feet), which delivers one of the best 360-degree views in the White Mountains despite not being recognized on the official AMC list of 4,000-footers (it lacks the necessary prominence). I relaxed here, possibly for too long. I just couldn't help it. The entire day's events, including two big climbs with an overloaded pack, caught up to me. I was gassed.

I eventually hiked down from Hight and reached Zeta Pass, a junction with the Carter Dome Trail. Route 16 is just 3.8 miles west from here. So, this spot offers hikers a chance to bail out and get off trail. While that didn't interest me, it was 6:30pm and starting to get dark. I knew the Imp Shelter was 4.8 miles away and now out of play. So, I sat on the Zeta Pass bench and decided I would cowboy camp (on the ground) at the first spot that looked right.

This was the Appalachian Trail after all, and hikers slept on it regularly. While on the bench, I got a visit from a pair of dudes. One mentioned something about the Yellow Deli, which meant nothing to me. It was an odd on-trail discussion that left me sort of scrambling to get moving toward the summit of South Carter (4,430 feet). It was just .8 miles north of Zeta Pass and it was next on my list. I reached the summit and just 100 yards or so further, there was a perfect camping spot carved out. It was nearly dark now, and I was happy to call it home for the evening. There was a stunning full moon that night, and it was silent up there. But I didn't sleep well. It wasn't the night I had planned for during the past six months. I was alone on the ground while my hiking partners were about 3.5 miles away in bunks after being served a warm dinner.

"The hut was kind of cool. The rooms were nice. Small, individual rooms," said Reimer. "We had dinner and breakfast. They had a telescope and a kid whose dad worked at NASA."

As I laid under the stars and moon thinking about the next day, I made the decision to cut my hike short. I had summited four 4,000-footers and would add the fifth, Middle Carter, in the morning. I had hiked 8.4 miles carrying 50-plus pounds and it just didn't make sense to continue on to Moriah solo. I could bail out via the Imp Trail and get to Route 16, shaving more than four miles off my total distance.

So, I was choosing to hike 14.6 miles and summit five 4,000-footers instead of hiking 18.8 miles and bagging six. This would also get me home to Carrie quicker and I had heard great things about the view of the Northern Presidentials from the Imp Face, a lookout on the Imp Trail. It was a great pivot for me.

Back at the Carter Notch Hut, the New Boston Dads were also putting together a plan for Saturday.

"We were hiking out," said Reimer. "We knew there was going to be some thunderstorm activity, we were dog-ass tired and there was no way we were going to be able to continue. So, we were going to hike out 19-Mile Brook Trail to Route 16 and somehow find our way back to the car.

"I think at the point we made that decision, we were all just collectively beat, combined with the weather, and there was a party Saturday back in New Boston we were considering."

Unger quickly chimed in, "But the door was always left open to continue. We said, 'Hiking out sounds great, but let's wait and see how we feel in the morning.'"

Reimer noted his disappointment as he tried to sleep in the hut that night.

"It didn't feel good, but it felt like the right choice when we went to bed," he said.

When I awoke on South Carter that morning, I packed up quickly and just before I departed camp, I realized my hiking poles were missing. But it made no sense. They weren't special or expensive. I paid $40 for them online. So, the idea someone stole them in the middle of the night was ludicrous. Plus, I am a notoriously light sleeper, and didn't sleep well that night. There was no way somebody tiptoed in and scooped them out from under my nose. No way.

Then I remembered the Yellow Deli guy, and how I abruptly departed that conversation. I must have left my poles at Zeta Pass, leaning against the bench I was sitting on. I was .8 miles from there and about 500 feet above it. I made the call to not go take a look. I didn't want to add 1.6 miles to my day for "starter" poles. I knew I needed to upgrade to better ones and this would fuel me. Plus, I'd learned a valuable gear lesson: always take inventory before moving on, despite the circumstances. Still, it was a tough way to start my day. Back at Carter Notch Hut, the New Boston Dads were about to start their day.

"Things felt different waking up. I woke up feeling good," said Reimer. "I was still lying in bed and I already knew I wanted to continue. Jake was the first person I saw in the morning. I told him I'd like to continue and he said, 'Same.' We were all aligned thinking let's do it. It was a good feeling especially after the night before which was a crappy feeling. We had built the trip up. I now call it the All-Healing Carter Notch Hut because it changed everything. That was a pivotal night's stay in my hiking career."

Reimer, who is from Buffalo, New York, officially launched an assault on Northeast peaks the following spring. He finished the NH 48 in the fall of 2015, completed his Winter 48 in 2018, and summited the 4,000-footers in New York by 2019. He also knocked off the remaining peaks of the New England 67 and New England Hundred Highest. His license plate reads "115ER," which represents completing all of the 4,000-footers of New York (48) and New England (67).

In the summer of 2022, Reimer was nearing the completion of the NH 48 Grid, which includes climbing every NH 48 peak during each month of the year (not in a single year). Finishing the grid means a hiker climbed 576 total NH 48 peaks (48 x 12). It is an astonishing accomplishment considering he was on the verge of hiking out after his first day, possibly retiring his boots with just five miles and two NH 48 peaks on them. However, he woke up feeling good and set his sights on reaching the Imp Shelter, which was seven miles from Carter Notch.

"That day's hike went pretty clean. Carter Dome was a big climb for us but not too killer as we all had fresh legs after resting and sleeping in the hut," said Reimer. "We saw the guy from the Yellow Deli up there. He wrote it in the sand on the trail. When we were talking, he said he saw a guy hiking with a bucket the previous night. We were like, 'Oh yeah, we know him.' You got some notoriety on that trip."

Yes, I was the guy with a bucket. It was looped on to the back of my pack. It was one of those white-plastic Margarita Big Buckets with the handle, lid, and spout. It weighs nothing and is great for transporting water from springs to shelters. It also made an ideal receptacle for group drinks. Just dump some Crystal Light powder into it, shake, and you have lemonade or iced tea on tap. I really liked it and it came in handy. It also led to the only trail name I ever had, "Bucket."

I would push on from South Carter that morning and quickly summit Middle Carter (4,610 feet). From here, I had just .6 miles to my bailout point, the North Carter Trail to the Imp Trail. And it was all downhill. I made quick work of the first 2.1 miles, which put me on the Imp Face, a killer outlook that sits directly across Pinkham Notch from the Northern Presidentials and Great Gulf Wilderness. In a world where few things live up to the hype, the Imp Face delivers. I called my wife from here and we got caught up. I told her I was 2.2 miles from the road and just needed to get back to my car to start the three-hour drive home. She was happy. I was happy.

I crushed the remainder of the Imp Trail and immediately started hitchhiking. My car was about five miles north at the Carter-Moriah Trailhead. Just about everyone driving north along Route 16 would be passing it. I got a ride immediately from a hiker shuttle service. Perfect. Within minutes, I was at my car and beginning my trek home. I was making good time. So, too, were the New Boston Dads, who had a great day on trail and reached the Imp Shelter.

"We almost didn't continue on based on the weather report," said Neefe. "In the end, we decided to go forward with the knowledge of an escape route a few miles up. We were all very glad we did and you were missed."

"It started to click for us on Saturday that we could do this. I gained confidence that wasn't there at all on the first day. It felt a whole lot easier. We were hitting our stride," said Reimer. "The Imp Shelter was crowded. There were several AT thru-hikers there. We had a great time. We had some scotch and that was part of the night's fun."

Added Unger, "It rained that night. Poured like hell."

I got home to Carrie, changed her bandages, and acclimated back to life off the trail. While I was only gone two nights, the transition back from the trail to work, computers, and certain responsibilities can be a bit of a shock. The New Boston Dads, well, they went on to finish their Wildcats-Carter-Moriah Traverse as planned. They summited Moriah and hiked out Sunday at Rattle River, where they had spotted a car. Despite the challenges, both Reimer and Unger look back fondly on this trip.

"I embrace it. I have told the story of this hike a few times. Last time I was on the Wildcats, I told it," said Reimer. "That was the pivotal point in my whole hiking journey. That hike. The agony. The pitfalls. The staying at the hut and making the decision to go on. If we didn't, if we hiked out, I don't know if I'd be hiking today. It's crazy. All those little memories hit me whenever I'm hiking over those spots. I think about those times and that hike. The events that went down. It's cool to draw upon those."

Added Unger, "The thing that sticks out to me the most about that hike is the weight we were carrying. We had packed like amateurs because we were amateurs. We had a ton of crap, way more than we needed. Starter gear, heavier gear."

Reimer noted that there's a certain stretch of trail that triggers one memory in particular every time he crosses it.

"There's a cool spot up on the Wildcat Ridge Trail, kind of an open area between Wildcat D and Wildcat," he said. "Every time I pass that spot, 11 times now, I remember we were all sitting on a log. We were trying to relax after our first summit. I remember thinking, 'I need to calm down.' I felt a little better. I was still sore as hell, but the hangover was passing."

Unger, too, has his memories.

"I remember loving the terrain, being so psyched to be there, and walking across the boardwalks, through some of the marshy areas, and thinking it was awesome," he said. "Just soaking it all in and thinking how cool it was. My takeaway remains the views and some of those cool sections."

As for Bucket the Hiking Guide, I was feeling guilty about putting my new friends in such an uncomfortable spot. It wasn't until I got the whole story in full detail on the rest of their hike that I finally felt good about it all.

"You were obviously an experienced hiker looking out for our best interests. You thought these guys can do 12 miles. I appreciated the aggressiveness," said Reimer. "The emails you sent really laid the foundation. It made me think our leader knows what he's doing. They began in March and April, and we had five to six months to get ready. And we did a good job on some levels. I got a ton of gear. Boots, backpack, sleeping bag, sleeping pad, headlamp. All this stuff specifically for this hike."

I asked Unger and Reimer to grade my performance as their guide.

"B, B-minus," said Reimer laughing. "Mostly for overestimating our abilities, which is not fair because we did not do ourselves any favors by drinking the night before or preparing by going out for any hikes beforehand. We didn't hold up our end of the bargain. I think it was aggressive but I also thought it was great. You introduced the idea. We were attracted to it. We said, 'Let's do it.' The planning was there. You tried holding our shit show together as we were falling apart."

Said Unger smiling, "I would agree, probably about a B or B-minus. You needed those peaks, that was part of it, so it was a little self-serving. But we all would have done the same thing. Having not done it before, we didn't know what those first miles were going to be exactly like. And while it was a hiking trip, it was also our first time away together and we were all excited to hit it that first night. So in retrospect, it was not the smartest move but we all signed off on it and it was a lot of fun."

## CLIFF NOTES: WMS CHAPTER 18

🚶 When planning a trip, build it with the least experienced hiker in mind.

🚶 Be sure to prepare your body (and mind) for a big adventure such as a multi-day hike.

🚶 Always carry a credit card, or extra cash, in case of an emergency. You can hide it in your gear if it makes you feel more comfortable.

🚶 Always check your surroundings after taking a break and moving on down the trail.

🚶 Beware of folks promoting the Yellow Deli, as it is linked to the Twelve Tribes religious cult.

---

**Facebook Post:**

Keith Gentili
September 7, 2014

ROAD TO 48 UPDATE (WILDCAT-CARTER RANGE)—If you ever skied Wildcat, you know the view from up there is, well, breathtaking. Here's a look from Wildcat as well as a few shots including Carter Lake and Carter Notch Hut from the climb to Carter Dome. Slept on South Carter Summit, then hit Middle Carter before hiking out Imp Trail, which provides a signature view of Northern Presidentials from its Imp Face; just 2.2 miles from Rt. 16 and a family friendly hike (note it). Total trip 15 miles, about 5,200 elevation gain, 27 hours on trail. 36 Down, 12 to go.

# CHAPTER 19
# Making Movies

Date: Friday, September 26, 2014
Mountain Range: Presidential
Peak/Elevation (feet): Jackson 4,052, Pierce 4,312
Route (Thru Hike): Webster Cliff to Crawford Path to
  Highland Center
Total Distance: 10.5 miles
Hiking Partner: Jason Unger
Road to 48: #37, #38

Just as I did during both my "freshman" year (The Kinsmans) and "sophomore" year (The Hancocks), I put a birthday hike on the calendar. I had to as I was building the completion of my entire NH 48 journey around finishing by my 48th birthday—September 27, 2015—that was now a year away. It also was a nice time to evaluate my progress each summer, kind of an annual report card as the hiking season was winding down. I targeted the Southern Presidential peaks of Mount Jackson and Mount Pierce.

Individually, these two mountains can be among the easiest 4,000-footers to climb for hikers taking them on as straight out-and-back treks. The summit of Jackson is just 2.6 miles from the Crawford Notch Depot, with a very moderate elevation gain of 2,152 feet. On November 19, 2019, I took my daughter Julia, then 18 years old and wearing Microspikes, to the summit of Jackson for her first 4,000-footer.

The direct route to Pierce features what is considered the oldest continuously maintained hiking path in America, the Crawford Path, as it dates back to 1819. This trail also has a very moderate grade and the summit of Pierce is just 3.1 miles from Route 302 in Crawford Notch.

However, I wasn't interested in those routes. Just as I mapped out the Willey-Field-Tom hike with a start at the Crawford Notch floor and a finish up top, this was my goal here. I had read a lot about the

Webster Cliffs and the aptly named Webster Cliff Trail. It was a longer, more extreme adventure featuring additional scenic overlooks as it brings hikers along the edge of the cliffs for a couple of miles. This became the plan and, it being a Friday, I had just one taker when the invitations went out.

"This was just three weeks after the Wildcats-Carters hike. I knew coming out of that hike that I had always wanted to hike the 48. I had talked about it, but it seemed like this unachievable thing," said Jason Unger. "But the idea of getting these two peaks in, after getting the Wildcats, Carters, and Moriah, would put me at eight of 48 and it was like 'Game On.' The drive didn't seem as long anymore and everything was coming into focus. That was a big part of it for me."

I picked up Unger in New Boston and we made the traditional stops in Goffstown to get supplies including gas, food, and drink. The drive was smooth and we were in Crawford Notch two hours later ready to get on trail. We parked at the bottom of Crawford Notch, elevation 1,275 feet, about a mile south of the Willey House site, which served as the trailhead to the Willey-Field-Tom hike (Chapter 12).

"It was a beautiful fall day. Just a bluebird day," said Unger. "We parked in the area off Route 302 directly across the street from the Webster Cliff Trail."

As we geared up and stretched out next to the car, we got a visit from a hiker coming off the trail. He was middle aged, had an accent, and was chatty. This section has the Appalachian Trail (AT) running through it and, during this time of year, September in the White Mountains, it's common for AT thru-hikers to descend upon New Hampshire. After a nice discussion about trail conditions, the state of New Hampshire hiking, and each of our plans for the day, we parted ways.

"We walked across the street, got right on trail, crossed the Saco River, and began climbing the Webster Cliffs," said Unger. "It's a cool trail. A lot of exposed rock and some scrambling. It was a lot different than we had done three weeks earlier along the Wildcats and Carters. I packed a lot smarter. It was a day hike so I was traveling much lighter. I definitely learned something coming out of that first hike."

*The 4000-Footers of the White Mountains* says, "This is the longest and hardest but most scenic approach to Mount Jackson, including a traverse of the spectacular Webster Cliffs and summit of Mt. Webster, with numerous views over Crawford Notch."

The footbridge over the Saco River was built in 2007 and provided us with a nice view upstream. The fall colors were dominant and we were both excited about the day. Then, we began climbing. The Webster Cliff Trail ascends quickly. At 1.1 miles, were at 2,075 feet. We continued to climb, thanks in part to the trail's switchbacks, for another .7 miles, where we got our first big view down into Crawford Notch. This was 1.8 miles in and at 3,205 feet.

"We got up to there and all the leaves were popping," said Unger. "We saw the leaf-peeping train cross the trestle and I got a picture of it. Just a prime fall day."

For the next 1.6 miles, the Webster Cliff Trail delivered. We went in and out of the forest, along the cliffs, got great views, and just frolicked our way to the summit of Webster (3,910). During this stretch, I noticed Unger taking a lot of pictures as well as setting a very nice pace. I knew it was going to be a full day on trail, and our two targeted peaks were still miles away. And while not a 4,000-footer, Webster has earned its way on the 52 With a View list.

"Looking down on the Mount Washington Hotel and the entire valley was cool," said Unger. "It was great to be up there and to see all that."

From the summit of Webster, we had 1.3 miles along the Webster Cliff Trail over to Jackson. It was a nice stretch and we were in a great mood as we neared our first 4,000-foot summit. Although, we had celebrated atop Webster for a little time, it was on the Jackson summit (4,052 feet) that we would really fuel up.

"We had lunch on Jackson," said Unger. "And took in that view of the Presidential Range and Washington."

It would be 2.6 miles before we reach Pierce and our day's final summit. However, in between our two peaks, sits the AMC's Mizpah

Spring Hut. This would mark my third straight hike featuring a hut (Chapter 17, Madison Hut; Chapter 18, Carter Notch Hut). Combined with the Greenleaf Hut (Chapter 1), Lonesome Lake Hut (Chapter 3), and Zealand Falls Hut (Chapter 15), this visit would mean my NH 48 travels got me to six of the eight AMC White Mountains high huts so far.

"We stopped at the Mizpah Hut," said Unger. "We got a brownie there, maybe some lemonade, and talked to the caretaker."

The Mizpah Spring Hut, elevation 3,800 feet, has a bit of a vacationland feel to it. Instead of big-mountains views to salivate over like some of its peers, there's a small green lawn for sitting. It's sort of a break from the mountains, designed for relaxing. We did just that before getting back on the trail for our final .9 miles to Pierce.

Unger continued to take photos throughout our adventure and he continued to set a nice pace. I felt comfortable with him taking the lead, as we were now more than seven miles into our hike. We reached the summit of Pierce (4,312 feet) cleanly and agreed it would be our final break of the day. We sat there for a bit, staring off at the majestic summit of Mount Washington. Assuming we would get down fine, Unger was now at 8/48 and I just hit 38/48.

Then, we banged out our 3.1-mile descent along the Crawford Path. Just like the day's first 7.4 miles, this section went smooth. As we reached the end of our hike, we saw the monument on a rock honoring the Crawford Path National Recreation Trail as "The oldest continuously used mountain trail in America." Unger took a photo, then we hopped out onto Route 302 and crossed the street. We found a patch of grass to sit on at the AMC Highland Center.

"When we got back down, you had to hitchhike back to your car," said Unger.

It's true. That was my plan. I told Unger I would hitch a ride to my car, as it was only four miles south along Route 302. I hitched a bit (possibly a bit too much) during my high school and college years, times when I was carless or my vehicle was broken down. I always thought of it as an adventure but it did come with its risks.

In the fall of 1985, I hitched from Fitchburg State to the University of Massachusetts for a weekend that included a Fools concert in the Orchard Hill Bowl. I got a ride all the way from Route 2 in Leominster from a dude on his way to UMass as well. It was a great night that ended the same way the following morning started, with Kate Bush's "Running Up That Hill" playing on a linear tracking turntable. We fell asleep with it on repeat, and it just kept playing. Some 36 years later, my daughter Sarah is hooked on the television show *Stranger Things* and Bush's "Running Up That Hill" is a cultural phenomenon.

I once hitched home after a closing shift at Lechmere in Framingham, Massachusetts. It was sort of a Best Buy of its day, a superstore of electronics, home goods, and sporting goods. It was during the summer before my senior year in high school. My home was about 11 miles away in Holliston but the direct route went through some bad sections of Framingham. I got picked up along Route 126 near the center of town and instantly got a bad vibe from the driver. He took me all the way into my neighborhood before he started asking me questions that I was not going to answer. As we went into a tight corner, the car slowed, and I jumped out. After a small tumble, I ran straight into the woods as I knew I'd find my own way home.

On this day, I knew folks departing the Highland Center were heading either north or south. I just needed to find some hikers heading my way.

"You got a ride in the back of a pickup truck from a couple who just finished their hike," said Unger. "They were in the parking lot and were headed in that direction. You just jumped in the back and 20 minutes later returned with your car."

We then began our return drive to New Boston with one more stop. I was getting pretty good at post-hike meals. The Woodstock Inn always delivered. Between brewing its own beers including a 4,000-Footer IPA, and a monster menu including Death By Sandwich and Death By Burger, we always left there satisfied. Black Mountain Burger in Lincoln was another spot that provided just what we were looking for after hikes—a great burger and IPA. I had also heard great things about Biederman's Deli in Plymouth. Word had it they made a great sandwich and poured killer craft beer.

We stopped at Biederman's. We drank Maine Beer Company's The Other One, which was fine but the place was swarming with fruit flies as we ate our sandwiches. It felt like the basement of my college apartment, without the fruit flies of course, and I loved that place. Just caught it on a bad day. I've been back since and it has been excellent.

"That hike was notable for me. It was the springboard for me to get to the 48. After that, my run of hikes started," said Unger. "The desire had always been there and it became real after that. I had heard about the 48 for a long time just from talking to people at work or whatever. For me, well before we ever did the Wildcats-Carters hike, it was something I was interested in. But it just seemed so far away and I never knew when I was going to get the time. All these different hurdles. By going up there and doing it, it made it all feel within reach."

Unger finished his NH 48 the following fall, just 13 months after the Wildcats hike when he and Reimer completed an early October Pemi Loop—a 30-plus mile loop that includes at least eight 4,000-footers. He would go on to complete the New England 67 a few years later. In the summer of 2022, he was close to finishing up his New England Hundred Highest. Unger also made a short movie of our Jackson-Pierce hike and posted it on YouTube. The first time I watched it, I was stunned. It was such a uniquely different contribution to my NH 48 journey than any of the Fitchburg State Hiking Club members had made.

"I'm not sure why I made it. Not sure what really spurned me," Unger told me. "I was taking a lot of pictures and I had the 48 bug at that point, which goes back to the whole decision we made at the Carter Notch Hut to go on and to get back out three weeks later on this hike. I stitched the pictures together that weekend. Then I put a soundtrack to it. It was just free music I found online to complement some of the pictures. It was the leaves, the train, a couple pictures of us, and some of the White Mountains-area signs. It was just over two minutes probably. It's still out there."

## CLIFF NOTES: WMS CHAPTER 19

🥾 Always have a plan to get back to your vehicle on a thru hike. Hitchhiking at this point in time is no longer a safe alternative.

🥾 Keep your pace but stop and smell the roses. Pictures chronicling your hike and views are a keepsake you may wish you had for family, friends, and the future you.

🥾 Perspective. While appreciating nature, respect history. From the Native Americans on the land centuries ago to a plaque revealing the nation's oldest hiking trail.

### Facebook Post:

Keith Gentili
September 27, 2014

ROAD TO 48 UPDATE (MT. JACKSON & PIERCE)—Got clearance from both bosses--work and home--to sneak in a birthday hike yesterday and targeted the southern half of the Southern Presidentials. Ideal weather and near-peak foliage made the 10.5 mile (3,800' of vert), 8-hour trek from Crawford Notch just spectacular. That's 38 summits down with 364 days to grab the final 10. PS Thanks for all the birthday wishes; very grateful for the warm thoughts.

# CHAPTER 20
# Embracing the Beauty

Date: Saturday, October 18, 2014
Mountain Range: Presidential
Peak/Elevation (feet): Isolation 4,003
Route (Out and Back): Glen Boulder to Davis Path
Total Distance: 12 miles
Hiking Partners: Keith Rice, Kevin Bell, Tom Fraser
Road to 48: #39

Just as Chapter 18's Wildcats hike introduced new hiking partners to my NH 48 journey, so too does Mount Isolation. In planning my October trip (and season finale), I reached out to two friends who traced back to high school, Kevin "Boog" Bell and Tom Fraser. I knew that they had both finished their NH 48 just a few years earlier and there had been some discussions about getting on trail together. It was something I really hoped could happen. I had good history with both Fraser and Boog and was excited about the prospect of hiking with them.

Fraser and I met in the winter of 1983-84 while working together at Lechmere in Framingham, Massachusetts. We were 16 years old, juniors in high school, and running wild in the stock room—searching for Technics turntables, Pioneer car stereos, and Sony television sets—at $3.70 an hour. After a few months, I got a promotion to the pick-up counter as management felt I was good with people and a microphone. It came with a 20-cent raise. Boom.

When I first met Fraser, he drove a killer candy-apple red 1971 Ford Mustang. We had both just gotten our licenses and, well, driving around in a car like that, at that age, was an event all its own. During one of our 15-minute breaks from stocking Lechmere's warehouse shelves, we went shopping for music. We wanted to parlay our 10% employee discount into some new tunes. We both love Pink Floyd. I bought two Pink Floyd cassettes that day, "Animals" and "Relics." I still have them and Fraser and I try to see a Pink Floyd tribute band together once a year.

While Boog and I first crossed paths just after high school, we began spending time together regularly during the early 1990s. We both had connections to Maine's Sebago Lake and spent endless summer weekends in the area visiting Sebago State Park, Trickey Pond, and Brandy Pond. In 2003, he played in the Gobble Gobble Horseshoe Tournament at my home in New Boston the day after Thanksgiving and hasn't missed one since. His homemade pulled pork and corn salsa are both showstoppers.

I have great respect for Boog and Fraser's friendship. In addition to hiking the NH 48 together, they also ski and camp a lot together. They've developed a trust, a closeness, and I believed it would be healthy to get on trail with them.

"We did 45 of the New Hampshire 48 peaks together," said Boog. "Some I did before Tom but then again with him. We were both single and getting out together was easy then. We had two other hikers in our crew but they got married before we started on the 48."

When Fraser and Boog confirmed for the Saturday, October 18 hike of Isolation, I was thrilled. As for the Fitchburg State Hiking Club members, while Engler and Hanson were not available, Rice was. Thus, we had a foursome, a date, and a mountain. We just needed to finalize the route.

"In planning, I was adamant about not taking the Rocky Branch Trail to the Isolation Trail," said Fraser. "The last time I hiked that, it was a flowing riverbed, which was not going to be good with the weather we were expecting that day."

This matched my thoughts. We were expecting some rain and, in reading trail reports on NewEnglandTrailConditions.com, the water crossings on that route were a legit concern. Plus, I was already leaning toward the Glen Boulder Trail to Davis Path. Not only did I want to see Glen Boulder, I liked the idea of hiking directly across the street from the Wildcats. In fact, the plan had us parking in the same Glen Ellis Falls parking lot off Route 16 used for the Wildcats hike. This route would also put us above treeline in Mount Washington's shadow at an elevation of 5,000 feet. Anytime you can reach 5,000 feet in the Whites, it's a good thing.

The four of us met at the Glen Boulder trailhead (elevation 1,975 feet) at 9:30am. I knew it was going to be a big hike, 12 miles total with two big climbs. I also knew we were going to get some weather, as rain and wind were in the forecast. What I didn't know was that Tom had a surprise in the car.

"Tom had his dogs with him," said Rice. "They were really well behaved."

While I had hiked with dogs here and there over the years, I had never climbed a 4,000-footer with a dog, let alone two. I was certainly not against it. In some way, I was looking forward to a new experience. Hiking with dogs has long been a sensitive subject on the 4,000-Footer Facebook groups. There are varying opinions about dogs being on leash or off leash. As a non-dog owner, who puts in about 200 miles per year on trails, I have come to believe there really are no bad dogs out there, but there are some bad dog owners.

"I had Ruby and Luca with me. Both are rescue dogs," said Fraser, who opted not to leash them during the Isolation hike. "They were both quite young and it was probably one of the longest hikes they had been on up to that point."

Ruby and Luca

During the first part of the hike, as we ascended quite steeply toward Glen Boulder, I spent a fair amount time with both dogs. It didn't take long to become enamored with and entertained by their enthusiasm. In short, they were fun.

"Luca was three-ish at that point, blind in one eye, and an extremely friendly husky-cattle mutt," said Fraser. "Ruby was a little younger, two-ish then, and a bit scared of people."

At the 1.6-mile mark, we reached Glen Boulder (3,729) and it was obvious both dogs were indeed well behaved. It was also obvious they were not going to have any trouble on the hike ("They seemed to be as energetic at the bottom as they did at the summit," said Rice.). We took some pictures there, including one of my NH 48 all-time favorites. It features Rice with his left hand resting on Glen Boulder with the Wildcats as the backdrop. He's holding his hiking stick in his right hand and the fog is oozing up from Pinkham Notch and dissipating into a wall of October red-and-orange foliage. It's great, and pure White Mountains State.

As we climbed our way toward the junction with the Davis Path, Fraser and I continued to catch up. We talked about hiking, work, our wives, and our families. There was a lot to get to and we had plenty of time. He noted that hiking wasn't the same for him in 2014 as it had been when he was finishing his 48 in 2010. He hoped this day could help change that but wasn't confident. Here's why, in his own words.

"In 2010, while on my way to meet Boog to hike and camp on Mount Garfield for our number 46, I called my brother. He didn't pick up, so I left a message. He returned my call but I was on the Garfield trailhead access road and out of range. He didn't leave a message," said Fraser. "Garfield was a great hike. We cowboy camped on the summit and hit Owl's Head the next day for number 47.

"Three days after I got home from that trip, I got the call my brother was dead. Life changed. Somehow, my brain associated hiking with that phone call. Hiking in the Whites now had a dark taint over it and it was no longer the same.

"Boog and I finished our 48 on Mount Carrigain on October 30, 2010. We camped one night and summited from the west side doing a big loop. It was sleeting and windy as we approached the summit. There was no view. I climbed the tower solo and cast a thimble of my brother's ashes in the wind. It was a crummy way to summit the final peak."

On November 11, 2020, Fraser and I set out to hike the White Mountains' 30-mile Pemi Loop. We spent two nights and three days together on trail and had another chance to catch up. This time, it was me who had recently lost a sibling as my brother Steven died December 31, 2018. He was 54. November 11 was my brother's birthday and we hiked nearly 14 miles that day, from the Lincoln Woods Visitor Center to the Mount Garfield Shelter. We summited six 4,000-foot mountains and got hit by a nice wave of rain and wind along the Franconia Ridge. We had the Garfield Shelter to ourselves that night and both spoke openly about our brothers' lives and deaths. It was therapeutic and cathartic.

"Our Pemi Loop trip was immensely helpful for me. I learned I was not alone. Your sharing your story meant a lot to me," said Fraser. "On our Isolation trip, I was in the process of selling my childhood home I inherited with my brother to help take care of his widow. I was not in a good frame of mind that day."

Rice, Boog, Fraser, and I continued up the Glen Boulder Trail. It was 1.6 miles from the boulder to the junction of the Davis Path and an elevation of 5,000 feet, where we'd be above treeline. During this stretch, the beauty of the area floored me. The pictures we got supports this. The combination of the fall colors, sporadic fog,

landscape, and plant life was jaw dropping. When we reached that point, we knew our first big climb was behind us. Just 3.2 miles from the car, we had already gained more than 3,000 feet of elevation. It was time for a break and some fuel.

"I remember having mini bagels with cream cheese," said Rice. "And eating them all day long."

One of this route's unique features is descending to the Isolation summit. Here we were at 5,000 feet just a tad over two miles south of the summit of Mount Washington and we needed to go down to claim our targeted NH 48 peak. Mount Isolation sits 2.8 miles from the junction of the Glen Boulder Trail and Davis Path, and 1,000 feet below it. With the exception of some blowdowns and enchanted woods type challenges, we ripped out the Davis Path with a purpose. Six miles from the car, we got our mountain.

"Isolation has a great view when the weather is right, but it wasn't that day," said Rice. "It can also be a pain in the neck to get to it."

We enjoyed the summit, and rested up. Our day's second big climb was ahead of us and, when we reached it, we would be seven-plus miles in. It was going to be a challenge. Plus, the weather we had avoided to this point was about to arrive. So, we got back on trail and made our way up the Davis Path. The first mile was moderate; the next two were a slog. It was raining lightly and the wind was starting to hit.

"At miles eight and nine," said Rice. "We still had 1,000 feet of vertical climbing. We got some wind and misty blowing rain.

Eventually, we were fully exposed, no tree cover. "

It was a tough grind for all of us. We just put our heads down and took it step by step. As we gained elevation, the cloud cover got thicker, the rain steadier, and the wind faster.

"It was dreary and rainy up there," said Fraser. "I don't remember there being a view of anything on the way back."

Tom Fraser

Yet, I couldn't help but feel surrounded by beauty. The images from our climb up were so fresh that I knew I was in a special spot during a special time of year. The fog, rain, and wind was somehow amplifying my attraction. I wasn't wet, hungry, thirsty, or lost. Tired? Sure, but that's part of the deal. And while we still had some climbing ahead of us, it was going to be 3.2 miles down the Glen Boulder Trail to the Glen Ellis Falls parking area and our cars. So, despite the seemingly never-ending ascent I was on, I couldn't help but embrace the beauty of the moment.

We reached the junction somewhat individually as we had separated a bit on the final-half mile or so. We took some pictures, shot a little video, and turned right to make our way down the homestretch. We reached the parking lot at 7:30pm, after 10 hours on trail covering 12 miles. My "junior" year was now over. I was at 39/48 and right on schedule.

"That was a tough hike for me," said Rice. "It's a long one, a monster hike. I was beat after it."

Isolation would mark the 18th peak that Rice and I climbed together on my NH 48. It was also our final one as he was unable to join me during 2015, my "senior" year.

"My family was busy in 2015. That was a tough year for me," said Rice. "I didn't get any hikes in. You invited me a bunch of times; they just didn't fit into my schedule."

I would join Rice on trail in the following years as he continued his NH 48 journey, ultimately finishing his NH 48 on November 8, 2020 atop Mount Carrigain. Engler and Hanson were also there that day to celebrate.

As for Fraser, he was reflective in 2022 when looking back on his White Mountains relationship.

"The point of time just prior to my brother's death in 2010 was the happiest I had ever been. Life was always an upbeat Grateful Dead or Phish song as I pretty much lived for hiking and skiing," he said. "These days the sky is blue again and the taint over hiking in the White Mountains is gone."

**CLIFF NOTES: WMS CHAPTER 20**

🥾 Sometimes you have to hike down to reach the top of the mountain.

🥾 Pink Floyd's "Animals" is still worth listening to once a month.

🥾 Beauty is always on trail; the key is being able to recognize it.

---

**Facebook Post:**

Keith Gentili
October 19, 2014

ROAD TO 48 UPDATE (MT. ISOLATION: 4,003)—Last 12 days have been a roller coaster and the Mrs. gave me a day to get in an October hike. It was wet/foggy/windy/cold/dark at times but overall just fine. Total hike: 12 miles, 5,000' elevation gain, 10 hours on trail (9:30am-7:30pm). No. 39 in the books.

# CHAPTER 21
# Winter Hiking

Date: Sunday, March 1, 2015
Mountain Range: Presidential
Peak/Elevation (feet): Eisenhower 4,760
Route (Loop): Crawford Connector to Crawford Path to Edmands
  Path to Mt. Clinton Road
Total Distance: 10.6 miles
Hiking Partners: Eric Engler, Ron Reimer, Jamie Neefe
Road to 48: #40

Although my NH 48 "Senior Year" may have officially launched on March 1 with the Eisenhower ascent, my 2015 hiking season kicked off on January 2. The New Boston Dads, including Ron Reimer and Jason Unger, were starving to get on trail during the holidays and experience winter hiking. So was I. Thanks to my Cabot and Waumbek adventures from the previous spring, I was comfortable working with them to come up with something. The plan? The Franconia Ridge Loop, the day after New Year's.

"We were reading trip reports leading up to it and we knew we wouldn't need snowshoes," said Reimer. "We knew we would need Microspikes. I went out and bought them as well as a ton of other winter gear."

After the Waumbek incident (see Chapter 14), I purchased Microspikes and was eager to strap them on. The Franconia Ridge Loop would be a great opportunity and test, as we would be climbing up the Falling Waters Trail (the reverse direction of my original Franconia Ridge Loop detailed in Chapter 1). This was sure to have us hiking on a ton of ice. We were all excited. Here's an email I sent on New Year's Day featuring a high-elevation weather report.

*From: Keith Gentili*
*Subject: Franconia Ridge Loop: Jan. 2*

*Date: January 1, 2015 at 4:20:27 PM EDT*

*To: Jason Unger, Ron Reimer*

*Here's some weather via TrailsNH.com for our loop. Certainly not meant to concern anyone; just being thorough.*

## FOR FRIDAY:

*A chance of snow showers between 9am and noon. Mostly cloudy, with a high near 11. Wind chill values as low as -19. Very windy, with a west wind 35 to 40 mph, with gusts as high as 55 mph. Chance of precipitation is 30%.*

FRIDAY: SUMMITS OBSCURED. A CHANCE OF SNOW SHOWERS IN THE MORNING. HIGHS AROUND 14... EXCEPT 4 TO 14 ABOVE AT ELEVATIONS ABOVE 5,000 FEET. WEST WINDS 35 TO 45 MPH... EXCEPT WEST 55 TO 65 MPH AT ELEVATIONS ABOVE 5,000 FEET. CHANCE OF SNOW 30 PERCENT. WIND CHILL VALUES AS LOW AS 34 BELOW.

As a reminder, the Franconia Ridge Loop includes Mount Lafayette and Mount Lincoln. These two summits are about a mile apart and both are higher than 5,000 feet. So, we knew we were going above 5,000 feet and heading into extreme winter conditions. But we were ready, and hungry to get after it.

"We got up there and on trail early," said Unger. "I remember it was snowing."

"We put our spikes on in the parking lot. It was 8am and windy," said Reimer. "There were only a few snow-covered cars in the parking lot."

The hike up Falling Waters was a blast. Thanks to our Microspikes, we all felt like billy goats as we climbed on, across, and over long stretches of ice. Our new form of traction made us all feel comfortable.

"Everything was frozen over going up Falling Waters. It was great and we got up to the ridge pretty easy," said Reimer. "It was your call to layer up before going above treeline and summiting Little Haystack. Every time I pass that spot I think, this is where we layered up on my first winter hike."

Added Unger, "We had a conversation about continuing across the ridge. The wind was howling. Visibility wasn't great. But during that conversation, it cleared a bit over Little Haystack and we made the decision to go on."

Reimer recalled his first taste of entering a winter alpine zone.

"When we first broke treeline, it just smacked us in the face. It got real, really fast. I remember asking you, 'Where else would you rather be than right here, right now?' It's a [former Buffalo Bills head coach] Marv Levy quote. It was a whiteout and I was loving it. But a few minutes later it cleared up for a little while."

As we made our way across the Franconia Ridge, the wind eventually picked up and visibility went down. Conditions worsened and staying on trail was a concern. I turned over the lead to Unger, who had no trouble keeping us on track.

"When we got up onto Lafayette," said Reimer, "I went from general excitement and just loving it to realizing that this is a real situation. That heading down to the Greenleaf Hut was going to take some work and locating cairns might not be easy."

Despite the deteriorating conditions, we weren't cold, tired, hungry, or thirsty. We were in good shape to start the descent.

"I'll never forget us getting face to face on Lafayette and you saying, 'This is not a survival situation,'" Unger told me. "I knew we felt good. I think we weren't discounting the weather but we were comfortable. We were about over it and just had to get down to the hut."

We took some summit photos on Lafayette and then began our trek down to the Greenleaf Hut by moving from cairn to cairn. One of us would proceed alone until they found the next cairn, and the rest of us would catch up. It was sort of a hiking version of follow-the-leader. We also had a GPS device that helped keep us on trail.

We weren't perfect but we got it done. I once mistook a small pine shrub covered in snow for a cairn, and the GPS alerted us we had strayed. We had to work our way back to the trail. We eventually ran into a group coming up from the hut and knew, at that point, we were golden. We followed their tracks and the trail right down to the hut where the conditions were fine. We got inside and fueled up on warm food and drinks. It was a nice celebration and confidence-builder.

"My takeaway was that we were all doing this together," said Reimer. "You were very stern about that. We couldn't separate. It was a great learning experience."

Two months later, Eisenhower was the target and more winter hiking was on the docket. The chosen route would include summiting Pierce and there was a good amount of snow in the White Mountains at this time. Thus, my run to get 40/48 would be another snowshoe hike and I was thrilled. My Microspikes had made their debut in January and now my new MSR Evo Ascent snowshoes would climb their first 4,000-footer. The invitations went out.

"I was in. I had the time off. This was going to be my 20th peak of the 48. When I saw 20, I realized I was starting to creep toward having 50 percent of them completed," said Engler. "I bought a bunch of gear for that hike. I got goggles and I finally bought a balaclava to cover my head and nose. So I was completely protected up there and I needed it."

Reimer and Jamie Neefe also joined the trip and the three of us departed New Boston together. We met Engler at the McDonald's in Lincoln on the Kancamagus Highway.

"It was the first time I met Engler," said Reimer. "He was playing Billy Ocean on his car stereo and I wasn't sure what to make of that."

176

It was a prank. Engler is pure classic rock, and most often listens to 1970s guitar rock (Deep Purple, Led Zeppelin, Grand Funk, etc.). We carpooled up to Crawford Notch and parked right off of Route 302 in the lot located at the end of Mount Clinton Road, which is closed in the winter.

"It was cold that day, way colder than temperatures I had hiked in up to that point. So I was nervous again," said Neefe. "But I had my group of friends, so it quickly vanished."

The day's route was big, 10.6 miles, and included going up the Crawford Path and coming down the Edmands Path. It would also take us over the summit of Pierce, which meant at the successful conclusion of this hike, I'd have four official peaks toward the Winter NH 48 (Lafayette, Lincoln, Pierce, and Eisenhower). However, completing that list—hiking the NH 48 between the winter solstice and spring equinox—was not on my radar at this time. The weather was nice, but cold. At 8:30am, we jumped right onto the Crawford Connector, elevation 1,920 feet, and got moving.

"Beginning to end, we were on snowshoes that day," said Reimer "It was a pretty smooth walk-up to Pierce. I was kind of getting to know Engler and I remember on the way up him saying, 'Hike your own hike.' That resonated with me and he ended up behind us. He was moving slow but that paced us and that was good. It allowed us to enjoy a nice leisurely stroll up in easy conditions. The Crawford Path was essentially a sidewalk."

"For me, meeting new people isn't in my wheelhouse," said Engler. "I don't make a good first impression. I don't say too much. I'm hard to approach and my first answers to questions aren't great because I'm not revealing much about myself."

The Crawford Path is known for its moderate incline and we enjoyed it that day. It was a smooth three miles up to our first summit.

"When we hit treeline, and the alpine zone," said Reimer, "it took me right back to being on the Franconia Ridge Loop on January 2 and that was great. I remember thinking this is where I want to be."

A fellow hiker took a great photo of Engler, Neefe, Reimer, and I atop the Pierce summit with a snow-covered Mount Washington as the backdrop. Each of them stands six feet or taller, while I'm 5-foot-9 on a good day. This was a bad day as I'm positioned just a bit behind them, and on the start of a slight downslope. The result is I look short in the photo, especially standing next to them.

"Remember that jockey who showed up and photo bombed us?" asked Reimer regarding that picture.

After a little time on the summit, we made our way toward Eisenhower. Despite the cold temperatures, it was a bright and sunny day. We had about 1.5 miles to the summit.

"We stopped and had some water and food in between Pierce and Eisenhower," said Reimer. "That whole stretch between the peaks seemed to go so fast."

It was between these two peaks that I found a small pink ski pole. I made the decision to hike it out. I figured I might be able to use the "Hike the 4000 footers of NH!" Facebook page to locate the owner. I had been pretty active on the page that winter and figured it was the right call. It worked. The pole belonged to Alex Herr, whose mother Trish is very active on Facebook. In addition to creating The Terrifying 25 with her daughters, Trish also wrote the book *Up* about hiking the 48 with Alex. It's an inspirational read especially for anyone with children. I met up with Trish a week later in Manchester, NH. As a thank you, she gave me a chocolate chip cookie the size of a Frisbee. It was another confirmation of the hiking community looking out for itself and another tremendous winter day on trail.

"Conditions were great that day. We summited Eisenhower [4,760 feet] and came off to the side to take a break," said Reimer. "We had one final beverage before taking on the Edmands Path."

"I remember the crazy winds on the top of Eisenhower," said Neefe. "And not hanging around too long."

We had hiked over five miles so far in nearly ideal conditions. The Crawford Path treated us well. It had been broken out clean and firm. We snowshoed on top of it without any issues. We had just .2 miles to the junction of the Edmands Path, where we turned left and traveled along the north side of Eisenhower.

"Right after we hit the Edmands Path, which had obviously not been as well traveled as the Crawford, it became very slow going," said Neefe. "We were breaking trail in 24 inches of fresh snow. Post-holing to the crotch. Falling sideways and throwing your pole to stop you. It was exhausting. I don't recall how far that went on for, but it seemed like miles."

"Once we turned and we got into the trees, we were post-holing in our snowshoes. The snowdrifts were just incredible and that's where we got introduced to spruce traps," said Reimer, of the risk of hiking on the tops of snow-covered trees and falling into them as the snowpack breaks. "We were often waist deep trying to dig ourselves out. The snow was high enough where we were in the trees, and even our faces were in the trees. It was nuts. All of our hikes to that point, the trees were above us. But we were actually in or on the tops of the trees this time."

Said Engler, "I'm the slowest hiker. I was behind you guys. You were directly in front of me and every now and then, you would fall in [a spruce trap] and yell, 'Ohhhh. What is happening?' as you went down and you weren't using your inside voice. You'd be struggling to get out and I was laughing. But then it would happen to me."

This cycle repeated itself for at least a half-mile or so as we made our way around Eisenhower and tried to get down off it.

"I can remember my entire legs going down into the snow, right up to my crotch. One foot was up and the other down. It was treacherous and exhausting. But I didn't realize at that time that we were walking in the treetops," said Engler. "I bent a pole on that hike, one of my starter poles, trying to get out [of a spruce trap]. I realized it was time to get rid of the cheap box-store poles and get good ones. Same with my snowshoes and goggles."

Neefe also had an issue related to his gear.

"I stopped to take a photo, and my glove fell off my pole and started sliding down a sheet of ice," said Neefe. "It went about 150 feet and miraculously stopped before dropping into the trees. I was thinking it would really suck hiking the rest of the way with one hand in my pocket. I gingerly walked down to retrieve it."

Eventually, we made our way off Eisenhower and into the forest. During this final stretch of the Edmands Path, we were walking through a winter wonderland. It was just gorgeous. The snow-covered trees built a canopy that reminded me of winter in Narnia.

"It became a lot better after we were fully in the forest," said Reimer. "And it was beautiful."

"There was such a feeling of relief when we finally got into the trees and the snow got shallow again," said Neefe.

The Edmands Path ends after 2.9 miles. With Mount Clinton Road closed, the parking lot was empty. We turned left and began the two-mile walk down the road to our cars. We were quickly greeted by the sounds of engines.

"Mount Clinton Road turns into a snowmobile trail in the winter," said Reimer.

"The last two miles on the road, I was pretty exhausted and just wanted to get back to the car," said Neefe.

When we finally reached the lot at 6pm, we were all spent. It had been a full day on snowshoes with a few big challenges. Pushing through the drifts really wiped us out.

"After this hike, I began to dig in on the New Hampshire 48 list," said Reimer. "I started to really think about it a lot."

As for Engler, he warmed up to Reimer after nine-plus hours on trail. The two had an engaging discussion on the final miles, in which I could often hear them laughing.

"I didn't know Ron, and we talked a lot on the way out, the walk down the road to the parking lot," said Engler. "We started by easing into conversations busting on you. You were our common thread. We were making fun of you. Because that's what we always do. It's a thing."

## CLIFF NOTES: WMS CHAPTER 21

🏂 Check and track multiple weather sources when winter hiking. It's imperative to stay updated on potential conditions including temperature, wind chill, precipitation, and wind gusts.

🏂 Always layer up before climbing above treeline. It can be extremely difficult to do this above treeline when wind and precipitation can run amok.

🏂 Be open to upgrading your equipment when you feel the timing is right. It can help you become a multi-season and more frequent hiker.

🏂 Be respectful of and contribute to the greater good of the hiking community. Opportunities to give back will find you someday. Seize them.

### Facebook Post:

Keith Gentili
March 2, 2015

ROAD TO 48 UPDATE (EISENHOWER, 4,760 FEET VIA PIERCE 4,312)—Got out Sunday to enjoy the mild temps (8-18) and snowshoe a chunk of the Presidential Range. We hit Mt. Pierce first but the big target was Eisenhower, our state's 12th highest peak and No. 40 overall for me. Total trip: 10.6 miles, 9.5 hours (on trail 8:30am to 6pm), 3,100 feet of elevation gain. Note: Some of the better photos here were taken by other members of the group.

# CHAPTER 22
# The Dog Days

Date: Sunday, April 12, 2015
Mountain Range: Carter-Moriah
Peak/Elevation (feet): Moriah 4,049
Route (Thru Hike): Stony Brook to Carter-Moriah
Total Distance: 10 miles
Hiking Partners: Eric Hanson, Eric Engler
Road to 48: #41

As the spring of 2015 rolled in, the higher elevations of the White Mountains were covered in a deep snow and my penchant for winter hiking was taking off. I set my sights on Mount Moriah for mid-April and began working on a route. I had originally planned to summit Moriah on the Wildcats-Carter Traverse (Chapter 18) but, well, not all trips go as expected.

After a good amount of research, I decided on a sort of thru hike. I would approach Moriah from the southwest and depart it to the northeast. This 10.7-mile route resembled a backwards "L." It started on Route 16 at the Stony Brook Trailhead and ended on Route 2 at Rattle River. This plan also provided a bailout on the Carter-Moriah Trail that would return me to Route 16 quickly and turn the hike into a slightly shorter horseshoe. Regardless of the trails, fresh snow was due to hit that week, so it would certainly be an adventure.

Then, I reached out to my hiking partners and filled them in. Both Hanson and Engler were in. I was thrilled. Weather was shaping up to be great and I began thinking we might hit a winter bluebird day.

"I met you at your house," Engler reminded me. "And we drove up together and met Hanson."

Engler and I scooped Hanson in Concord at the I-89 Park & Ride off exit 2. The three of us then made the long drive north through Franconia Notch and Twin Mountain, past Appalachia, and over to Gorham. The Stony Brook Trailhead (elevation 960 feet) is about two miles south of the village of Gorham along Route 16. We arrived a little after 9am and began gearing up and stretching out. It was bright and sunny as we strapped on our snowshoes. At 9:30am, we got on a smooth, broken-out trail.

We had a few water crossings and a moderate ascent during the first two miles. The forest and valley were just beautiful that day. It's worth noting that winter hiking features leafless trees. This allows for longer views in the woods. Winter hiking also means no bugs and, if you dress properly, minimal sweating. Even the trail itself is easier to navigate as the terrain's rocks and roots are often covered by a clean snowpack. After crossing Stony Brook at 2.3 miles and 1,850 feet, our climb really began.

"I remember when it started getting steep because I was wearing my new MSR snowshoes," said Hanson. "And I remember thinking, these things are awesome. The hike up, all the way to the ridge, was pretty straightforward."

We reached the junction of the Carter-Moriah Trail at 3.6 miles and 3,127 feet. The three of us were in a nice groove as we arrived on the ridge and the weather was cooperating.

"I felt I was coming into my own at that time," said Engler. "Rice had questioned my Swedish wool sweater on the Cabot hike. He asked me why I was carrying that when there are other options that are so much lighter. But I knew what worked for me despite it not being new, fancy gear like puffy jackets."

We turned left on the ridge and headed for the Moriah summit. We had 1.4 miles to our peak, and this section of trail delivered a series of outstanding outlooks that combined to provide views in all directions. We were having a great day on trail and our summit was coming up fast. We reached Moriah's highest point (4,049 feet) five miles from the trailhead.

"I was impressed by the view from the Moriah summit. It was a sunny day and I had never seen Mount Washington from that angle. It was awesome. It was a different perspective, and it really struck me on that hike," said Hanson. "North of there is nothing in terms of the White Mountains. It was interesting to be on the edge, the northeast edge, of the range and the region."

We spent nearly two hours on the summit of Moriah. Hanson was in charge of lunch. He had a plan and fired up his cooking gear.

"I made parmesan tuna fish and noodles," said Hanson. "But I had forgotten you guys didn't like that stuff. Engler was like, 'Nah.'"

"Hanson tried to serve us his Charlie Tuna, Chicken-of-the-Sea noodles meal," said Engler. "I'm not eating that. I would never eat that. I'd rather put some hot dogs or beef stew in my kid's thermos. I ate a can of beans on one of the 48s and some Chef Boyardee on another, but I wasn't eating that."

Despite Hanson's lunch snafu, we were rocking the summit and had plenty of other fuel. We also had the peak to ourselves for a long time. The view of the snow-capped Northern Presidentials was just so rewarding it was hard to leave. Then, two big dogs arrived. They were overly friendly and made their presence known. They made the rounds a few times looking for food, pouncing on us, and essentially getting into our stuff (including my trail mix). It quickly became a problem. We scrambled to put our food away and somewhat organize our gear.

"The frolicking pups," said Hanson. "I remember the owners were on the older side."

About five minutes after the dogs arrived, their owners showed up. They assured us their dogs, a collie and golden retriever, were friendly, which they were. However, that didn't diminish the chaos the tandem created. We continued to pack up and made the decision to depart. In short, these two overly friendly dogs ran us right off the summit and onto the Kenduskeag Trail.

Height of the sign shows the depth of the snow

"We tried to make a run north toward Shelburne Moriah but the trail wasn't broken out," said Hanson, who can be seen in a photo looking down on the Kenduskeag Trail sign thanks to the high snowpack. "We could see the blazes on the trees, and we tried. But we immediately got in up to our waist. We were tripping over logs. It just wasn't meant to be. The snowpack was probably four feet deep or so. And it had snowed recently, so it was soft. We fought it for about 20 minutes and that was it."

We dug ourselves out, turned around, and began our descent on the Carter-Moriah Trail, the bailout plan. We had 2.5 miles to reach the summit of Mount Surprise (2,194 feet) followed by another two miles to the trailhead and Route 16, where I would hitch a ride south about 1.5 miles to the Stony Brook Trail parking area. We soon caught up to the older couple and the dogs. Despite our best efforts to be friendly during small talk, the dogs continually jumped on us with unbridled enthusiasm. It wasn't really a problem but I feared the conversation was at risk of getting snarky and began moving us along.

We continued down the trail to the summit of Surprise and it delivered just a stunning view of the Northern Presidentials. We stopped here, took some photos, and had a round of cold drinks. The sun was bright and the sky was an unmistakably winter blue. It was a

great moment and we embraced it, knowing our next stop was pavement.

"Then our hiking buddies show up," said Hanson, as the two dogs eventually came racing down upon us. "They were our new friends."

Again, it wasn't a problem. In fact, it became quite comical. The dog owners arrived minutes later just as they did on the summit. We had a nice, sincere on-trail discussion about the view and the conditions before they continued down. Then, I got an idea. I told Hanson and Engler that it only made sense to time my arrival at the Carter-Moriah Trail parking area with that of our new friends. Then, it would only be natural to ask them for a ride back to my car. I even thought things could play out in a manner such that they offered me a ride before I asked.

"Yes," said Engler. "That's your ride."

After another 15 minutes or so, I split from my hiking partners and began to work to catch up to the very dogs that had been haunting me since the summit of Moriah. It was pure irony, the exact opposite situation of what I really wanted. But I put a push on the final mile of trail and did indeed catch up to the party of four. The dogs were thrilled to see me and we all rolled into the trailhead area together. Being 6pm on April 12 with a bunch of fresh snow, there was only one car in the parking lot, a blue Subaru Forester.

"Where's your car?" asked the gentleman.

"It's about a mile and a half down Route 16 at the Stony Brook Trailhead. We went up that trail and then across the ridge to Moriah," I replied.

"You want a ride?" he asked.

I was relieved. It happened naturally and I wouldn't have to hitch. Then, I had this instant vision of sitting in the small backseat area with those two dogs. They would be all over me. Ugh.

"Do you have room? I don't want to impose. I'm not sure you have room," I replied and, in the moment, I believed it.

"Get in the car. Take the front seat," he replied, and suddenly all in the world was right.

And so, I rode shotgun and placed my pack between my legs. I also made a decision to not push the seat back. It was up when I climbed in and it didn't seem fair to slide it back as the wife sat behind me with both dogs to her left. As we pulled out of the parking area and took a left onto Route 16, I felt good. Between our conversation on the final section of trail and the insistence to join them, I was now genuinely relaxed in their company. Plus, I just completed a 10-mile hike and climbed a 4,000-footer on snowshoes. I was tired.

As the Forester began getting up to speed, it happened. The golden retriever hopped over the console separating the bucket seats and moved on top of me. I was stunned. And thanks to my pack being at my feet, the dog was truly in my kitchen. He quickly wriggled himself so that we were chest-to-chest, and face-to-face. The dog owners seemed amused by this turn of events. I was in disbelief and working toward shock. Then, he began to bounce, rhythmically, on me.

Somehow, I felt this was karma. After all, it was my plan to be in this car at this moment. And here I sat, being humped by the same dog that ate half my trail mix on the summit. Perhaps this was just the price of the ride. Whatever the case, I knew we only had a mile to go. There was nothing I could really do. I was trapped in the Subaru's cockpit. I did my best to fight off the advances but, in the end, was forced to sort of ride it out. Just as we arrived at the Stony Brook Trailhead, like clockwork, the dog returned to the back seat.

I got in my car and made my way back to Hanson and Engler, who I found sitting on the curb, enjoying a beverage, and yukking it up. Seems they were having quite the giggle while a canine was assaulting me. When asked about this moment, Engler was quick to note his affection for his hiking partner.

"He's a sweetheart, Hanson. His personality is just fantastic," he said. "We hiked a lot together and he hikes so much faster than me. He would often be ahead of me, get up a knoll or find a high spot, and wave back to me. Then, once he had my attention, he would kick a leg up and break into the air guitar. He's so awesome."

## CLIFF NOTES: WMS CHAPTER 22

🏂 Embrace winter hiking as the views can be better thanks to leafless trees. Plus, there are no bugs and minimal sweating.

🏂 Always check with the chef before getting on trail or you risk staring down a parmesan tuna fish and noodles summit lunch.

🏂 When possible, plan hiking routes that provide a bailout that shortens your total distance and gives you options.

🏂 Beware, riding in cars with dogs can be ruff.

---

**Facebook Post:**

Keith Gentili
April13, 2015

ROAD TO 48 UPDATE (No. 41, Mt. Moriah 4,049)—Got out yesterday and got some sun in the White Mts. Moriah sits at northern end of Wildcat-Carter Range which still has about 4-5 feet of snowpack on top. Total trip: 10 miles (all snowshoes), 3,400 feet of elevation gain and one step closer to wrapping this up. Just four hikes left and seven peaks.

# CHAPTER 23
# 42

Date: Sunday, May 3, 2015
Mountain Range: Presidential
Peak/Elevation (feet): Monroe 5,372
Route (Loop): Ammonoosuc Ravine to Crawford Path to
  Gulfside to Jewell
Total Distance: 10.4 miles
Hiking Partners: Eric Hanson, Eric Engler
Road to 48: #42

In the spring of 1996, I made my debut on the Tuff Stuff Publications softball team. I selected uniform #42 in honor of Jackie Robinson and settled in at third base that season. The team had some talent and made a playoff run that, like most playoff runs, came up short of a championship.

Based in Richmond, Virginia, Tuff Stuff published a variety of national sports collectibles magazines as well as a slew of related special issues ranging from fantasy sports to NASCAR to non-sports trading cards. I moved from Massachusetts to Virginia on Halloween 1995 for a role on the editorial team and it quickly lived up to my expectations of being a dream job. My travels took me a host of great events including Super Bowls, All-Star Games, and the National Sports Collectors Convention.

On April 15, 1997—in honor of the 50th anniversary of Robinson breaking baseball's color barrier—Major League Baseball Commissioner Bud Selig announced the league was retiring uniform #42. Selig noted April 15 would forever be known as Jackie Robinson Day and players currently wearing #42, such as Mo Vaughn of the Boston Red Sox and Mariano Rivera of the New York Yankees, would be allowed to continue to wear it until their retirement. I wrote a piece about Jackie Robinson Day for the magazine. When the Tuff Stuff softball team issued uniforms that spring, without asking, I was given #42. Seems I, too, was grandfathered in. It was an honor and I wore

#42 for another two more softball seasons for Tuff Stuff, including one championship year.

In April of 2015, I began making plans to hike Mount Monroe, which would mark summit 42/48. I made the decision that the route would also include climbing Mount Washington, Monroe's neighbor 1.7 miles to the north. The plan was to replicate the 2006 Outdoor Adventure hike that delivered my first NH 48 peak along with the Monroe addition. The idea of returning to the Washington summit, to sort of pay tribute to where it all started, was a draw. Hanson and Engler, who were both with me that day in 2006, signed on. And based on the reports we were seeing, we knew it would be another snowshoe adventure.

"I questioned you on the plan," said Hanson. "Why are we going up Washington? We don't need it. What is this, a fitness thing? Why are we making it harder for ourselves? Washington is still a decent climb from the Lakes of the Clouds Hut."

As always, I saw value in taking the bigger route. In addition to honoring our prior hike, I wanted to stand in the snow at an elevation of 6,288 feet. I wanted to stare down into the Great Gulf from the summit of Washington. If we only climbed Monroe, we would not get that adventure. The added mileage would most certainly be worth the experience. Yes, the juice would be worth the squeeze.

"I didn't look at the first peak, Monroe, as the challenge," said Engler. "I looked at the whole hike as a challenge. My goal that day was to get up to Mount Washington, even though Monroe was the one we needed."

We parked at the Cog Railway (elevation 2,500 feet) just after 9am and headed for the Ammonoosuc Ravine Trail. The three of us moved efficiently that day. For me, it was my fourth White Mountains winter-conditions hike of 2015 and I had a system. For someone who 13 months earlier had never been on snowshoes, I had become very comfortable on them. I also had found a rhythm to my winter clothing layers. I wasn't the only one.

"On the OA hike of Washington in 2006, the weather was not good and I wasn't dressed appropriately," said Engler. "From the pictures of the Monroe hike, I could see I was comfortable in my clothing and I recall my gear worked out great for me. I had a routine that I was accustomed to at that point."

We reached the Lakes of the Clouds Hut, 3.1 miles from the car, without any issues. The hut sits at an elevation of 5,012 feet and the day's hike was right on schedule. We had a short ascent, .4 miles, to Monroe's summit and ripped it out. There was a small celebration with a summit beer and lunch. During this time, I removed my outer shell and unveiled a navy blue #42 jersey. There is a great picture of my back, sporting a bold white number 42, as I'm staring up at a snow-covered Mount Washington. To our surprise, Hanson too had brought something unique on this hike.

"I brought my bike lock all the way up there," said Hanson. "For no reason, of course. I forgot it was in my backpack. A little extra weight to carry and Engler just had to take a picture of me with it while we were on Monroe."

Hanson and the bike lock

After a nice break on Monroe's summit, we returned to the Lakes of the Clouds Hut and began our ascent of Washington. The conditions were ideal and picturesque. We were able to drop a layer as we made our way up the snowfield.

"I know we did fine on the way up to Washington but it was a bit of a struggle for me," said Engler. "I think I was surprised there wasn't more snow up there."

"On the way up to Washington, heading for the summit, we saw all those skiers and snowboarders. That was awesome for me," said Hanson. "I've only skied Tuckerman Ravine. I never saw anyone ski other parts of Mount Washington. We met a French guy. He was older, and he was a guide. He had huge skis. He was a true alpinist. He had a young couple as clients that day. I remember thinking how great that was. When we were on the summit of Monroe, it looked like skiers were going everywhere. That was really exciting. But then, they were all gone and we had the whole place to ourselves."

We reached the top of Washington, and we really did have the summit to ourselves. It was sort of empowering. Everyone we had seen or met along the way was now gone. We were able to have a nice little photo shoot at the summit sign. Hanson even found time to give his fans, Engler and I, a little air guitar.

"We were blessed to be on the summit alone, at that time," said Engler. "It was a nice change from last time I was there in 2006 for the OA hike. We could hang out, take pictures, and relax."

Despite being alone atop Washington, we made the decision to not take an extended break there. Rather, we would start our descent on the Gulfside Trail and find a spot on the edge of the Great Gulf to hang out for a while. There is a genuine feeling of remoteness along that section of trail. It's vast and has a sense of the wild about it that's undeniable.

"We were headed for the Jewell Trail and stopped on the edge of the Great Gulf and basked in its glory," said Hanson. "I loved that."

"We got very lucky. We had a great view all day," said Engler. "Those pictures on the edge of the gulf are spectacular. We all took a ton of pictures. It was a such a great day."

It was along the Great Gulf that we slowed down and embraced our day's work. We had snowshoed more than six miles, climbed two

big mountains, and it was downhill from here. The car sat in the Cog Railway parking lot, four miles below us, and we had nothing but time to enjoy the moment. We even got to watch a train make its way along the Cog Railway tracks.

"It was one of the most beautiful hikes I've ever been on. The views were great," said Engler. "In terms of winter hiking, that was a standout for me. A favorite."

"At that point of the game, there was a lot less suffering," said Hanson. "That's really the best way to put it. We were at our peak then. Full stride, running around with the alpinists. We had snowshoed other mountains. We knew what to expect. We had better gear and we were fully experienced. We were 'seniors' and relishing it."

We began our final leg of the descent and, like most of our adventures, we had made a full day of it. We returned to the parking lot in the dark at 8pm. We hung around for a bit, enjoying the solitude of the parking area. It had become part of my cycle, essentially tailgating in the lot after the completion of each hike. It was part of the reward for completing the assignment. I liked putting on dry clothes and comfortable shoes for the drive home. But I also like not being in a rush to start driving.

"That was a big hike," said Hanson. "But we were in good shape at that time, and we sort of crushed it."

"After this hike, I felt 'I got this.' My confidence was really there," said Engler about the NH 48. "It was the combination of climbing these two big mountains, on snowshoes, and it not being one of the most challenging hikes I had done."

For me, #42 was now in the books and I was looking ahead to the end of the NH 48 road. I knew it was time to begin formulating an exit strategy. Mount Carrigain, as originally planned back in 2012, would be last. Owl's Head, a 20-mile, single-peak journey, was likely going to be next. That left four remaining summits—Garfield, Galehead, South Twin, and North Twin. These mountains are positioned consecutively at the northern end of the Pemigewasset Wilderness. They set up nicely for an overnight trip and that was on my mind in the Cog Railway parking lot that night. For Hanson, however, he was still reveling in Engler's performance on the Monroe-Washington trip.

"Engler was hilarious on that hike. Classic Engler. His commentary on the way to the summit of Washington was great," said Hanson. "You were ahead of us at one point and he was just zinging you. He ran with the why-are-we-climbing-this-mountain theme. He kept saying, 'We've already climbed it.' We were having such a laugh. I'll always remember laughing with Engler, a lot, on that one."

## CLIFF NOTES: WMS CHAPTER 23

🥾 When the weather cooperates, be sure make time to sit still and embrace the beauty.

🥾 Read the body language of other hikers, and if they want to engage in conversation, take advantage of it. Learn from others.

🥾 Don't be in a rush to get home. The adventure doesn't always end when you reach the car.

---

**Facebook Post:**

Keith Gentili
May 4, 2015

ROAD TO 48 UPDATE (NO. 42: MONROE 5,372 FT.)—Got out Sunday and knocked off our state's 4th highest mountain. We also shot up Mt. Washington (6,288 ft.) as it sits just 1.7 miles from Monroe's Summit. Not sure the photos will do this one justice as the weather was ideal. Total trip: 10.4 miles with 4,200 feet in elevation gain in 10.5 hours (9:30am to 8pm; yep. we took our time).

# CHAPTER 24
## Five Guys

Date: Saturday, August 1, 2015
Mountain Range: Pemigewasset Wilderness
Peak/Elevation (feet): Owl's Head 4,025
Route (Out and Back): Lincoln Woods to Franconia Brook to
  Lincoln Brook to Owl's Head Path
Total Distance: 18.4 miles
Hiking Partners: Eric Hanson, Eric Engler, Jason Unger, Ron
  Reimer
Road to 48: #43

Everything about the Owl's Head hike was a little different. Even the peak's name is unique, as it doesn't include the word "Mount" or "Mountain." While I wouldn't say there was a lack of enthusiasm in putting together this hike, there was a marked lack of excitement. Plus, my NH 48 journey was winding down, and this allowed me to take both June and July off as my exit strategy was coming to fruition.

I had two hikes remaining after Owl's Head, and they were both on the calendar. The plan called for an overnight trip on August 21-22, which would include a stay at the Garfield tent platforms and four 4,000-foot peaks: Garfield, Galehead, South Twin, and North Twin. Then, on September 26, the day before my 48th birthday, Mount Carrigain would be the finale. That would have me waking up 48 years old on September 27 as a 48er. I liked the sound of that. But for now, the focus was on Owl's Head, and the trip was lacking some buzz.

"The thing about Owl's Head is that it's kind of boring. The hike is so long and there's not a lot of rewards," said Hanson.

"That trail went on forever," agreed Engler.

"Owl's Head was the one hike where all of the feedback online indicated the only reason to hike it was to check the box. I wasn't sure what to think about that going in," said Unger.

The summit of Owl's Head is nine-plus miles from the Lincoln Woods Visitor Center. The hike is not noteworthy. The ascent is not significant. The view is...well, there is no view.

"It was our single longest day on trail at that point. It was just a lot of miles," said Reimer of the 18-plus mile trek. "It was good to get that one behind us."

It was this attitude among all of my hiking partners that made planning the Owl's Head hike unlike any other trip. I came to realize that our route and our target would not be providing the magic. It would be up to us, the participants, to do that. So, I pushed members from both of my hiking groups—the Fitchburg State Hiking Club and the New Boston Dads—to commit to the trip. The result? We got five guys: Hanson, Engler, Unger, and Reimer all signed on.

"We never did have six," said Hanson, as Rice was unable to join us on this day and throughout 2015.

"That was my first time meeting Hanson," said Reimer. "He was a cool cat right from the start."

The plan was to meet at the Lincoln Woods Visitor Center around 9am. We would gather there, take inventory, and stretch out before crossing the 160-foot suspension bridge that spans the East Branch of the Pemigewasset River.

"I remember Engler couldn't get into the Lincoln Woods parking lot," said Unger. "It was overflow parking and he ended up on the Kancamagus Highway about a quarter of a mile east."

The rest of us were able to park in the main lot. We geared up knowing we had a challenge ahead of us. It would be a full day on trail and the combination of personalities had me encouraged.

"We got a 10am start. I snapped a picture of us crossing the bridge at Lincoln Woods," said Reimer, who also noted Owl's Head would get him to 28/48.

We hit the Lincoln Woods Trail and began our hike at an elevation of 1,160 feet. The first three miles of this route is as close to a walk in the park as the White Mountains offer. The trail is wide, thanks to its former life as a railroad track. There are still a lot of ties along this stretch and we hit them going out and coming back.

"I call it the Railroad Hike," said Engler. "I remember somebody leaving their bike down there."

200

It is not uncommon to see a bike parked at the end of the Lincoln Woods trail. Although hikers may not be aided by a bike when working on the NH 48 per AMC rules, there are plenty of folks out there working on other deals choosing to pedal those first three miles before pursuing adventure in the Pemigewasset Wilderness.

"I do remember walking along those railroad ties," said Hanson. "They seem to never stop."

At 2.9 miles and at an elevation of 1,440 feet, the trail splits. We went left on the Franconia Brook Trail. As a party of five, we began hitting our stride through this nondescript section. A rotating series of pairs and trios would form with conversations ranging from music to mountains to beer to sports. All the while, we were making tracks. At 4.6 miles (1,760 feet), we turned left on the Lincoln Brook Trail, which features a series of river crossings that can present an issue pending the water levels, weather, and time of year.

"The river crossings weren't too challenging that day," Reimer recalled. "In fact, I don't remember a lot of the details before the slide."

"We had a few river crossings and we were gauging where we were on the trail by them," said Engler.

We continued along the Lincoln Brook Trail in search of the eight-mile mark. This would be our turn onto the Owl's Head Path, a rockslide that would lead us to our summit.

"There was a little cairn there at the time," said Reimer. "Sometimes that cairn is taken down by rangers because the path is not an official trail. But it was there for us. Hikers put it up. Rangers take it down."

The cairn sat at an elevation of 2,560 feet. We turned right onto the path and began climbing straight up. The first .3 miles ascends 740 feet. From here, we got a great view of the Franconia Ridge across the valley.

"As we were heading up the slide, the sky started to darken and it started to rain," said Reimer. "We put on our outer shells. We were able to kind of get off the slide and into the trees. There was a little thunder and lightning."

The path continued steeply for another half-mile. We hit the ridge 8.8 miles from the car. The path angled left and we made our way toward the summit. The new summit.

"You noted they changed the location of the actual summit," Hanson reminded me. "We had to hike in about another two-tenths of a mile."

At 9.2 miles, we reached our destination—the top of Owl's Head (4,025 feet)—and we were happy. It had been a long hike with few highlights. For me, Owl's Head marked the fifth and final time my NH 48 peak number (#43) matched its elevation ranking (#43). This had also happened on Washington (#1), Bond (#14), Hancock (#21), and Moriah (#41).

"In our summit photo, we had raincoats on. It's a unique, viewless summit," said Reimer. "It was a long trek and fun to celebrate. It helped having the Erics there."

"I remember being on the summit in the rain," said Unger. "And on the walk back toward the slide, we ran into that crew."

"Yes, we bumped into that group all wearing jeans," said Hanson. "Some of the guys had no shirts on and they were soaking wet from the rain and a girl had fallen in at a river crossing. They were trying to light wet wood and make a fire right in the middle of the trail. They were a mess."

After some conversation between the two parties, and advice that was not being taken, we moved on. I wanted to get back on the slide and take in that view of the Franconia Ridge. It was one of the few visual rewards this hike offered.

"That was a cool view of the ridge and much of the west side of the Pemi Loop," said Reimer.

It was a great spot for the five guys to spend some time together. We had a beverage and just soaked up the sun, which had now arrived in force. During our discussion, we tallied up our NH 48 group total and it came out to 169 peaks (43, 42, 31, 28, and 25). We talked about the AMC ceremony the following spring with the plan that all five of us would be there to receive our scrolls. Engler called it "the dance," as in "I hope to see you at the dance."

"From that spot, we could see also that big cliff all the rock climbers know how to get to," said Hanson.

With nearly nine miles ahead of us, we knew we had to start our return. It was going to take some work and we had to get after it. Just as it was on the hike in, the hike back didn't present any trail magic. Just good conversation and hiking partners becoming more and more familiar with one another. We churned out a big chunk of mileage before finally taking a seat.

"We stopped at one of the river crossings and took our boots off," said Reimer. "We let our feet soak. I had a bunch of blisters. My legs and feet were feeling it."

"It was a nice spot for a break," said Hanson. "It had a flat rock and sandy part to stand in."

We got comfortable for a bit. But, inevitably, we had to keep on moving. As we reached the junction of the Lincoln Woods Trail, during the bridge crossing over Franconia Brook, I took a group selfie. It's something I rarely did, especially in 2015. I wanted to capture the moment of the five of us on trail together before it was dark. I made everyone squeeze into the shot. I love that picture. We had hiked 15-plus miles at that point and our faces show it.

We finished crossing the bridge and started our 2.9-mile walk along the Lincoln Woods Trail and its railroad ties. Nighttime officially arrived.

"It got dark and that woman came running by us," said Unger. "We saw her headlamp approaching us and weren't sure what it was. She was lost or late for something."

Added Hanson, "She was running to and fro and we were wondering what she was doing. She was looking for someone I think. She passed us a few times and never said anything. It was weird."

We also didn't say anything. It just didn't feel right as she clearly wasn't seeking our assistance. She disappeared into the darkness and we continued our way down the homestretch, about two miles from the parking area. We each settled into our own pace thanks to a combination of exhaustion, pain, and desire to get off trail after 18-plus miles.

"I was delirious at the end of that hike," said Engler. "You guys were ahead of me. I kept thinking if I fell down, I was in trouble. I had headlamp problems. I couldn't see 20 feet ahead of me. My headlamp was over my hat and it was making a strange circling shadow, confusing me. I had to change the setting. I couldn't figure out where I was going. I was exhausted."

We completed our Owl's Head trip at 9pm, 11 hours after it began. It was real dark. We were real tired.

"We hit Engler's trunk on the Kancamagus for a final drink," said Unger. "For a single day, a single peak, it was a great hike. Just the mileage alone was noteworthy."

Engler remembers it for another reason.

"I was only nervous twice while hiking the 48," he said. "I was nervous when Hanson and I were together finishing the Madison-Adams hike and we weren't with you and we got off course. And this time, during that final stretch."

### CLIFF NOTES: WMS CHAPTER 24

- 🚶 Some hikes are about the people, not places. Cherish your hiking partners.
- 🚶 Your feet are your tires and blisters are a big deal. Always be prepared to battle them from the moment you sense a hot spot. Moleskin is your friend.
- 🚶 Check equipment before hikes when you know you'll be using it, such as a headlamp (batteries, fit).
- 🚶 Big mileage means a big commitment. Be sure to understand your objective every time out.

**Facebook Post:**

Keith Gentili
August 2, 2015

ROAD TO 48 UPDATE (OWL'S HEAD)—This one was more about the people and the distance than the mountain as five of us churned out nearly 20 miles Saturday to peak bag Owl's Head. We ran into a thunderstorm near the summit but still got plenty of sunshine and great views of the Franconia Ridge's east side. Total time on trail: 11 hours with 3,000 feet of elevation gain. No. 43 on the board.

# CHAPTER 25
# The Mountain Lion

Date: Friday-Saturday, August 21-22, 2015
Mountain Ranges: Franconia, Twin
Peak/Elevation (feet): Garfield 4,500, Galehead 4,024, South Twin
  4,902, North Twin 4,761
Route (Thru Hike): Garfield to Garfield Ridge to Galehead to
  North Twin Spur to North Twin
Total Distance: 15 miles
Hiking Partners: Eric Hanson, Eric Engler
Road to 48: #44, #45, #46, #47

Unlike the widespread indifference leading up to the 18-mile march to Owl's Head, there was high-octane momentum surrounding this trip. I knew I wanted one last NH 48 overnight adventure, and true to form, I ran with this idea straight to fruition.

The date was set early, and both Hanson and Engler committed from the get-go. The plan included 15 miles over two days and four 4,000-footers: Garfield, Galehead, South Twin, and North Twin. We would sleep at the Garfield Ridge Campsite tent platforms. This early, front-end execution provided us with a few weeks of fine-tuning in terms of planning food, drink, and gear.

"If there was any one hike during the New Hampshire 48 that epitomized the Fitchburg State Hiking Club, it was this one," said Engler. "We had enough supplies to rock up there for a couple of days."

The three of us drove separately, meeting at the parking area at the end of Haystack Road off Route 3 in Bethlehem. It was here that our hike would end the following day (I estimated we'd be done around 8pm). We left Engler's and Hanson's cars there. I drove us to the Garfield Trail parking lot off Gale River Loop Road, where our hike began, at elevation 1,500 feet.

"It rained a bit. The Garfield Trail has a nice clean grade all the way up, almost five miles to the ridge," said Hanson.

"It was misty on the first day and I had too much weight in my pack on the hike to the tent site," said Engler. "At that point, my pack was 52 pounds, more than I had ever carried. But I also knew once we hit the platform, I wouldn't have to carry it again."

It was 4.8 miles to the Garfield Ridge Trail with a vertical gain of 2,680 feet. Despite full packs, the ascent was generally comfortable. We did get some rain, but we moved efficiently and reached the ridge without incident.

"But we goofed at the junction," said Hanson. "We should have gone right up to the Garfield summit from there. We decided to go down to claim a tent platform, get set up, and then come back to the summit without our packs. But it was straight down from there."

The junction of the Garfield Ridge Trail and Garfield Trail is equidistant to the Garfield summit and the Garfield Ridge Campsite. It's .2 miles in both directions. What makes this spot (elevation 4,180 feet) so unique is that both destinations are also a similar change in elevation. The summit (4,500 feet) is 320 feet above this point while the campsite (3,900 feet) is 280 feet below. In short, this .4-mile stretch of the Garfield Ridge Trail—from the summit to the campsite—drops 600 feet. It's the kind of trail that can rob your body's energy.

"I was exhausted when we got to that platform," said Engler. "We also hadn't eaten at that point."

We arrived at the Garfield Ridge Campsite and grabbed a tent platform. We dropped our packs and got comfortable fast. That meant spreading out, as well as fueling up on food and drink. We had filled our water bottles at the spring on the way in, so we really had everything we needed for the night, except we didn't summit Garfield. A meeting was then held. To summit, or not to summit?

"I was totally supportive of the decision to not go back up to the summit," said Engler. "I had just changed into dry clothes."

So, we got busy having fun. We had a great spread of food and the bar featured all of the regulars: Hanson's plastic bottles of Jim Beam, Engler's 94-proof premixed rum and cokes, and my Nalgene bottles were now filled with Hard Arnold Palmers (vodka, lemonade, iced tea). The weather had cleared. The music was playing. We were hittin' the note on the Garfield Ridge tent platform and had nothing but time.

"Then that California couple showed up and set up next to us," said Hanson. "She was a crazy-hippie type and he was a film producer. And she was cold, so I gave her my jacket, which she was grateful for. The next morning she said I couldn't take it back, and I didn't."

Added Engler, "We were feeding them drinks all night. They were happy and taking weight from us."

And so it went for hours. The five of us just ripped it up. It was a special night as it sort of represented the NH 48's "last hurrah." This trip was moving me to 47/48 and the plan was already set for a Carrigain finale, which was going to be a simple day hike.

"That was one of the biggest party nights we ever had up there," said Hanson. "Which made the next day's epic 10-mile trudge even more difficult."

We did go late that night. When it was finally time to turn in, Engler found himself in a new situation.

"I had a new 30-degree sleeping bag that comes down to a point. A mummy bag. That when you roll over, it rolls over," he said. "I could not get comfortable and kept rolling around and making noise. You started yelling at me, 'What are doing over there? Could you stop?' It was so funny."

Although we may not have gotten much sleep that night, we slept great all morning. Same for our neighbors.

"We slept late—until 11am," said Engler.

"It was hot when we finally got up," said Hanson. "And we had to go summit Garfield."

Another meeting took place. We decided to have a quick breakfast—coffee with Pop-Tarts—then just get after it. We would peak bag Garfield, return to the campsite, and pack up. It made sense but we knew that 600 feet of elevation gain and the subsequent drop on the return to start the day would not be easy.

"It was a beautiful, hot day. It was also the most hungover hike I ever had to do," said Engler. "It was great, though. It was pretty epic."

We got it done. We grabbed our summit, returned to the tent platform, and made lunch while packing up. As a group, we were in rough shape. So, too, was the California couple as they had retreated to their tent for a nap. It was classic Fitchburg State Hiking Club, finally strapping on our packs around 2pm and getting on trail. We had 10 miles ahead of us and three more 4,000-footers. Next stop, the Galehead Hut, 2.7 miles away.

"I remember going down and up and over the Garfield Ridge Trail to Galehead and how hard that section was. It was just brutal," said Hanson. "When we got to the Galehead Hut, it was already getting late. It was like, 'Damn, we're only here.'"

The Galehead Hut (3,780 feet) allowed us to freshen up our water bottles. It was hot and we were in a battle to stay hydrated. It also allowed us to slackpack the half-mile to the Galehead summit.

"I remember being so thankful we could drop our packs at the hut for that climb," said Engler.

We reached the viewless summit (4,024 feet) and turned around. To say it was uneventful would be an understatement. We got back to the hut quickly.

"There was no ceremony on Galehead," said Hanson.

Now we faced our biggest climb of the day. South Twin is just .8 miles from the hut but it rises more than 1,100 feet. During our time at Galehead, we met a bunch of AT thru hikers. It was fun hearing their stories and they were certainly interested in hearing from us locals.

"They were coming from Georgia. We were coming from Garfield, just one peak over, and they had so much less gear than us," said Engler. "That stuff always floored me. How prepared they were with so little gear. They were passing us on the climb up South Twin."

We reached the summit of South Twin (4,902 feet) where the view was outstanding. We had continued conversations with thru hikers and there was a real celebration on this peak. It was another pure White Mountains State moment.

"Being up on South Twin that day, that was special," said Hanson. "It's a special place, and it was my favorite part of that hike."

The trail splits here as the AT goes south toward Mount Guyot and the Zealand Falls Hut. We went north toward our final peak of the day, North Twin (4,761 feet). It was 1.3 miles away and the ascent wouldn't be nearly as difficult as its brother or our hike's first climb, Garfield.

Engler, me, and Hanson

"There's a little cave up on North Twin that I had camped in a long time ago. It was good to see that again," said Hanson. "It was twilight as we were coming down, around 8:30pm."

The descent of North Twin is long. It takes 2.4 miles just to get down off the mountain and reach Little River at an elevation of 2,350 feet. It was dark now and we had been on trail for more than eight hours. We made our way down wearing our headlamps. We hiked through the heat and the hangovers, carrying somewhat heavy packs up and down four summits. We were feeling it. From the river crossing, we still had 1.9 miles to the car and we were ready to get out of the woods.

"I knew it was late and we were behind schedule," said Engler. "Typical struggle."

It was about 9:30pm as we began our way down this final section of trail along the river. I was leading with Hanson behind me. Engler, as he traditionally did, was trailing steadily. We made sure we could always see his headlamp and that we could always hear him. Every so often, one of us would yell something to confirm we were in range of each other and we would keep moving.

"Then we misread an arrow on a tree," said Hanson. "From the trail description, we thought we had just a half-mile out to the car. But we had another mile and a half or so and it messed with our heads."

That was the start of my first official mental meltdown on trail. I continued to lead for another 10 minutes or so, but I was struggling to keep us on trail.

"It was nighttime, we were discombobulated, and you kept following drainage runs into the woods," said Hanson.

It's true. My headlamp just kept picking up the drainage runs and I'd walk right down them and into trees. This happened repeatedly, ultimately leading to my collapse. I made Hanson lead after that. I needed to check out and just focus on following him.

It was now pushing 10:30pm and, despite knowing we were on the correct trail, I just couldn't believe that the cars were anywhere in the area. I certainly didn't believe we were about to walk up on them. I was also worried about Carrie, and what she might be thinking. My refrigerator note had us returning to our cars around 8pm and I was never this wrong. It became my single toughest mental challenge during the NH 48.

"I would agree," said Hanson, who was essentially in it with me as we took turns leading during the final stretch. "But the physical challenge was also kicking in. I kept thinking, how much longer do we have?"

Behind us, however, Engler was calm.

"I wasn't worried on that hike," said Engler. "I was exhausted. It was a combination of lack of sleep the night before, and hiking a ton of tough miles that day."

Then, we popped out of the woods and onto the north end of Haystack Road. We made it out. It was nearly 11pm and I was relieved.

We said our goodbyes quickly. Hanson got into his car and headed east toward Twin Mountain and North Conway. Engler and I went west toward the Garfield Trailhead, my car, and Route 93. We didn't have cell phone service yet, and while our hike was over the adventure was not.

Here is Hanson's account of his drive home that night.

"I was physically exhausted and at risk of nodding off. So, I pulled my go-to move and stopped at the Hannaford in Ossipee. I just couldn't drive anymore. It usually worked like a charm. I got about a half-hour nap, woke up, and pulled out of there. It's 1:30am or so and as I'm driving, I'm thinking it's really dark tonight.

"I get a few miles down the road and there's a police car. I see it, slow down, and the blue lights come on. Why is he pulling me over? The officer comes up and says, 'You know your headlights are off?' Ah, I start telling him my whole story of the hike. Meanwhile, he reaches into my car and turns the headlight knob to on. I'm still talking and he cuts me off, wishes me luck, and sends me on my way. I made it home but that one was tough. Hannah was worried as we were so behind schedule."

For me, once we got cell service my phone started pinging. Carrie had called me three times and texted me. And, as expected, each call had an elevated sense of urgency. The first call was around 9pm, and just a simple check in. The second call, an hour later, she expressed some concern. The final call, another hour later, she was upset and wanted to hear from me. It was now around midnight. I was following Engler toward Franconia Notch and was able to call her. I apologized for being so late and behind schedule. She was relieved and we hung up quickly. All that was left to do, or so I thought, was drive home.

Then I saw Engler brake hard and swerve. Here's his account of what happened.

"We passed the Lafayette Place Campground and I thought I saw a dog run onto the highway in front of me. But I also thought I could be delirious. I hit the brakes and noticed that the dog had a really long tail, really long. I thought it was a mountain lion. I slowed down and sort of moved into the breakdown lane. That's when a cub ran out across the road in front of me. Then I knew I had seen a mountain lion and its cub. One after another, I almost hit both of them.

"You and I texted about it. I decided to pull off at the rest area and sleep for a while. After I woke up and got back onto Route 93, a police car passed me on the left and flashed his blue lights at me. I might have been going too slow. I don't know.

"The next day I started making calls to New Hampshire Fish & Game to report my mountain lion sighting, and its cub. I made a few calls and spoke to a few people. In talking with them, I learned a little about the patterns of mountain lions. I also came to believe the state doesn't acknowledge or deny the presence of mountain lions in New Hampshire due to lack of physical evidence. But I'm 100-percent sure I saw them."

## CLIFF NOTES: WMS CHAPTER 25

🥾 Always try to summit the mountain on the first opportunity as planned. You just never know what obstacles might come later.

🥾 Take advantage of slackpacking; that little break from carrying weight can return some pep to your step.

🥾 When the going gets tough, lean on your hiking partners. They are your most important piece of gear.

**Facebook Post:**

Keith Gentili
August 23, 2015

ROAD TO 48 UPDATE (The Big Push: Nos. 44-47)—Got out this weekend for an overnighter. Five miles Friday in rain to Garfield (4,500 feet) followed by 10-mile hike out Saturday via Galehead (4,024), South Twin (4,902), and North Twin (4,761). Got late start Sat AM, which made for late night on trail (until 10:45pm) and got home after 1am. But 47 down and 1 to go...

# CHAPTER 26
## See You at the Dance

Date: Saturday, September 26, 2015
Mountain Range: Pemigewasset Wilderness
Peak/Elevation (feet): Carrigain 4,700
Route (Out and Back): Signal Ridge Trail
Total Distance: 10 miles
Hiking Partners: Eric Engler, Jason Unger, Ron Reimer
Road to 48: #48

"You actually planned to finish the 48 on the day before your 48th birthday when you started this whole thing back in 2012?" asked Reimer.

Yes, I did. It was always the plan, going all the way back to the Fourth of July, 2012, when I first discovered the New Hampshire 48. The goal was to wake up for the first time as a 48-year-old man and be a 48er, one who has climbed up and down all 48 mountains in New Hampshire with an elevation of 4,000 feet or higher recognized by the Appalachian Mountain Club. Part of the drive was based on being a resident of the state, a hiker, and being New Hampshire proud.

However, that plan was based specifically on a six-month hiking season. I figured, hiking once per month from April to October, it would take four full seasons (2012-2015) to get there. The game really changed when winter hiking became a part of the equation. In the end, I got ahead of that schedule and was able to somewhat coast to the finish line in an effort to complete my trek on September 26, 2015.

"The plan that day was to meet you and the New Boston Dads at your house early that morning. That was a bit stressful for me," said Engler. "I didn't want to arrive late and be the 'Fitchburg guy' messing everything up. Hiking with Hanson, who was always late and unreliable, I knew what that meant and didn't want to be that guy. It was stressful."

Engler wasn't late. He pulled into my driveway just before 6am, which was our meet time. Reimer and Unger had already arrived and the four of us set off for my final hike of the NH 48. I was driving and we were headed for the Signal Ridge Trailhead in Bartlett with our ultimate destination being the summit of Mount Carrigain—the center of the White Mountains, where up to 43 other 4,000-footers can be seen

"I was psyched for you on that hike. Your enthusiasm was infectious. We were like the folks walking behind Forrest Gump. We're walking because you're walking," said Engler. "It's because of that enthusiasm, the preparation, and how into it you were—I wish I remembered more than I do. I wish I were more conscious and present on more of the hikes. I wish I had stronger feelings about the trails. It's a regret of mine."

The drive to the trailhead was fun. We were in a festive mood and the celebration was officially launched somewhere along the way. It couldn't be stopped. We had momentum. We reached the Signal Ridge Trail parking area (elevation 1,480 feet) off Sawyer River Road and got on trail fast.

"I was so excited about that hike. It's number 48! The other guys were really excited too," said Engler. "I got on trail with you. Here we go, number 48. And boom, you guys take off. That was the fastest five miles I've ever hiked. Hands down."

But the start wasn't really perfect. Well, I should say, I wasn't perfect from the start.

"We were on trail at 9:07am and about a minute in, you took a header and went down hard," Reimer told me. "Here's big Mr. 48; excuse me sir, have you hiked before? It was hilarious. I recall that vividly. You went down and I was thinking this is going to be a good time."

I picked myself up and we did move swiftly along the trail, especially the first 1.7 miles, which has little elevation gain. It's here the trail splits, as the Carrigain Notch Trail enters from the right and the Signal Ridge Trail continues to the left.

"You were on fire. The New Boston Dads were on fire," said Engler. "I was blown away by that. Even your last hike of the 48 was still a challenge for me, as you guys were moving fast."

Not long after the fork, we began our actual ascent of Carrigain and the pace slowed a bit. We stopped at a couple of viewpoints along the northern end of the Signal Ridge Trail that are just spectacular. Then, the fire tower came into view and reality began to set in that my NH 48 journey was coming to an end. It was bittersweet, as I had really relished the entire journey from the planning, the packing, and the preparation to the driving, the trail talk, and the hiking including all the ups and downs.

"It was a very memorable moment," said Engler. "But you guys got there before me but had to wait, which worked out great for me as I arrived a little later and didn't have to hustle up the stairs."

Eventually, the call from the tower came. It was our turn. My hiking partners allowed me to summit alone. The uniqueness of the moment was highlighted by another hiker who can be heard on Reimer's video yelling, "He's the third one in the last hour!"

"It seemed like an easy hike up. There was great anticipation," said Reimer. "When we got the summit call at 12:28pm, I played 'Chariots of Fire' on my phone as you were heading up the steps. I was genuinely excited. This whole four-year journey was about to conclude."

I got up on the tower and quickly dug a New England Patriots T-shirt out my pack that had the number 48 on its back and the name "Peaks" above it. I had it made the previous month at the Pro Football

Hall of Fame in Canton, Ohio, while on a business trip. The store there offers custom T-shirts and jerseys. I just felt that shirt represented me well. I was a Patriots season-ticket holder and the Patriots were the current NFL champions. This hike was sort of my Super Bowl. I needed to be in uniform and, well, this is what I came up with.

"When you got on the tower and changed into your 48 Peaks shirt," said Reimer, "I was like, 'Where did this come from?' It was cool."

"I liked the '48 Peaks' shirt reveal," said Engler. "I'm not a New England Patriots fan but as a New York Giants fan, it was the best Patriots shirt I'd ever seen."

"That's the piece I remember, the T-shirt," said Unger, a lifelong Denver Broncos fan. "I was trying to figure out what it meant. It was cool."

We were fortunate to spend more than an hour and a half on the tower. We took a bunch of photos and our celebration spilled into another group's 48 ceremony. It was an as-good-as-it-gets moment.

"It was a beautiful day and we were on a great peak," said Unger. "There were a few other folks celebrating with us."

"There was the young woman who had just finished her 48 as well," said Reimer. "She had a sign and you took a picture with her."

Engler was also celebrating this summit while looking forward to his own conclusion.

"Carrigain marked my 39th New Hampshire 48 summit. I was busting them out at the time," he said. "I was into it and my idea was I gotta make it to the dance. That's what it was all about for me. I'm going to the dance."

The "dance" in this case was the AMC's annual spring awards ceremony celebrating the hikers who completed their respective lists the previous year. To be invited to the dance, one had to not only finish the necessary hikes but also complete an application—which included an essay detailing the journey—and have it approved by AMC staff. In short, it was a serious process, as the AMC certainly isn't handing out scrolls/diplomas without confirming the coursework was completed.

Engler wasn't the only one on the tower that day thinking about the NH 48 through a wider lens. Reimer, too, had an interesting experience on the top of Carrigain.

"There was a woman in her 70s on the summit that day and it impressed me so much," said Reimer. "At that point, I hadn't thought about climbing mountains at that age. We talked a lot and she told me all about her favorite hikes and how much she loved the Franconia Ridge. It changed my view."

After much merriment, we left the tower and began our descent down the Signal Ridge Trail. We had five miles to go to get back to the car and a plan to keep things rolling at Schilling Beer Company in Littleton. It just so happened the brewery's Oktoberfest was that night, and who doesn't love a Bavarian oompah band? But first, we had to get down.

"I remember hanging on to trees on the way down," said Unger. "My hands were covered in pine sap from using them to hold me up."

Added Reimer, "The weather that day was crazy nice. It was just awesome, even on the way down."

We did make it down safe and we did make it to Schilling. There was outdoor seating (picnic tables) and a big white tent with an oompah band. The timing was serendipitous, but we were more than happy to roll with it. Schilling was also celebrating its second birthday and we were celebrating my 48th. We loaded up on pretzels and pizzas.

"It was funny that we ended up in Littleton," said Unger. "That was a good time."

At one point, I made my way under the big white tent and told the band that my 48th birthday was just hours away and that I had just finished the NH 48. I got some obligatory smiles and nods. Then, the music started and I began to dance a bit. Oompah music is not necessarily designed for dancing, so I returned to the table.

We soon loaded up and hit the road. I was driving my hiking partners home. Reimer was the first to fall asleep. Then Unger, who was riding shotgun, began the traditional head-bob and it was only a matter of time until he was going to be out. I did my best to trumpet it was my day, my birthday, and I wasn't going to be driving three sleeping corpses back to New Boston.

"I know I didn't fall asleep on the way home," said Engler. "I'm sure we were listening to some power trios and I was probably filling your ride home with some pure verbal nonsense."

Engler did indeed stay up with me for the drive. He's always good about that. The ride home, like the entire day, was pure Type 1 fun.

"That was your finish. It was exciting to see you complete the journey and we were eager to do the same," said Reimer. He and Unger started their NH 48 on the Wildcats-Carter-Moriah Traverse (Chapter 18) and finished on October 1 atop Bondcliff as they completed a Pemi Loop.

"We had hiked with you a bunch," said Unger. "It was good to be with you to finish it off."

Engler was reflective on his role in my NH 48 adventure.

"I was blessed to be there," said Engler, who in the summer of 2022 was at 93 in pursuit of the New England Hundred Highest peaks. "I was thrilled to see you eat the cake, and I was happy to be a sidekick on your journey."

## CLIFF NOTES: WMS CHAPTER 26

🚶 Set hiking goals and work toward them at your pace. Hike your own hike.

🚶 Like life, not all miles on trail are created equal.

🚶 Embrace hiking solo and cherish your hiking partners.

🚶 Never try to dance to an oompah band.

---

**Facebook Post:**

Keith Gentili
September 26, 2015

ROAD TO 48 CELEBRATE—After four years and 27 hikes, I am happy to report that I wrapped up the quest today by getting up Mt. Carrigain, which sits in the middle of the White Mts and is the state's 13th highest peak. Special thanks to all of the folks who hoofed it up there with me at some point along the way including Eric Hanson, Eric Engler, Keith Rice, Jake Unger, Ron Reimer, Jamie Neefe, Len Wolfe, Kevin Bell and Tom Fraser. At last I'm an AMC 48er. Here's looking forward to the banquet in the spring.

# NEW HAMPSHIRE 48
## In order of completion with date

**1. Washington, May 20, 2006**

*Freshman Year*

2. Lafayette, May 18, 2012

3. Lincoln, May 18, 2012

4. Flume, August 12, 2012

5. Liberty, August 12, 2012

6. North Kinsman, September 23, 2012

7. South Kinsman, September 23, 2012

8. Moosilauke, October 21, 2012

*Sophmore Year*

9. Tecumseh, April 27, 2013

10. East Osceola, May 5, 2013

11. Osceola, May 5, 2013

12. Zealand, May 16, 2013

13. West Bond, May 17, 2013

**14. Bond, May 17, 2013**

15. Bondcliff, May 17, 2013

16. North Tripyramid, June 22, 2013

17. Middle Tripyramid, June 22, 2013

18. Whiteface, July 31, 2013

19. Passaconaway, July 31, 2013

20. Jefferson, August 23, 2013

**21. Hancock, September 27, 2013**

22  South Hancock, September 27, 2013

23. Willey, October 27, 2013

24. Field, October 27, 2013

25. Tom, October 27, 2013

*Junior Year*

26. Cabot, April 6, 2014

27. Waumbek, May 4, 2014

28. Hale, June 7, 2014

29. Cannon, June 12, 2014

30. Adams, August 9, 2014

31. Madison, August 9, 2014

32. Wildcat D, September 5, 2014

33. Wildcat, September 5, 2014

34. Carter Dome, September 5, 2014

35. South Carter, September 5, 2014

36. Middle Carter, September 6, 2014

37. Jackson, September 26, 2014

38. Pierce, September 26, 2014

39. Isolation, October 18, 2014

*Senior Year*

40. Eisenhower, March 1, 2015

**41. Moriah, April 12, 2015**

42. Monroe, May 3, 2015

**43. Owl's Head, August 1, 2015**

44. Garfield, August 22, 2015

45. Galehead, August 22, 2015

46. South Twin, August 22, 2015

47. North Twin, August 22, 2015

48. Carrigain, September 26, 2015

**Bold represents peak number climbed and NH 48 elevation ranking match.**

# APPLICATION FOR THE FOUR THOUSAND FOOTER CLUB
## OF THE WHITE MOUNTAINS

The top of Mount Carrigain delivered. It was a stunningly beautiful fall day and, along with my three hiking partners, we summited the tower at 12:28pm on Sept. 26, 2015. I chose Carrigain because of its location in the center of the Whites. In less than 12 hours, I would be turning 48 years old and this is where I had long dreamed of spending this day. In fact, it had been precisely 1,179 days since I decided to stand here, in this exact place on this exact day.

My mother is always sending me weird stuff in the mail from Florida such as laundry detergent samples, women's cosmetics coupons (for the Mrs.), and odd newspaper clippings about big alligators on golf courses. But one day in March 2012 she mailed up a random copy of *Backpacker* magazine. I say random because it was dated May 2009. I read it. All of it; gobbling up the 96 pages of content like a Gray Jay attacking crackers atop Mt. Willey. One sentence in the cover story *America's 100 Best Dayhikes* changed my life; "Get a taste of the Alps in New Hampshire on this high-wire loop." It was under the heading Best Alpine Hike, Franconia Ridge, NH. Oh, I was hooked.

I hiked the Franconia Ridge Loop May 18, 2012. My group went up Lafayette, over to Lincoln, and down Falling Waters. While I'd been hiking my entire adult life (Shenandoahs in Virginia, Vermont, and Maine), other than Mt. Washington in 2006, this was my first taste of the 48 although I didn't know it yet. I just knew something was pulling me along that ridge towards Lil' Haystack but more importantly towards something bigger. I soon got my answer.

Six weeks later, at a Fourth of July party in my hometown of New Boston, I got into a conversation about hiking. It was here, on this day, that I first learned of the 48. I made up my mind then, instantly and without hesitation, I would complete the 48 on the eve of my 48th birthday. This would give me four years to do it. I got this. I knew it.

My plan: one hike a month from April to October knocking off regions. In the fall of 2012, I wiped out Franconia Notch. In 2013, the Sandwich Range. In 2014, the North Country and the Wildcat-Carter

Range. All the while, I'd chip away at the Presis. Things really opened up for me when I discovered snowshoeing. While it now seems like a natural evolution, I had no snowshoe experience. Cabot, Eisenhower, and Moriah were all snowshoe conquests. Plus, on Jan. 2, 2015, I took on the Franconia Loop Ridge a second time using Microspikes and reversing direction.

These four years (and 27 hikes) can be easily compared to high school. Everything was new and unknown during freshman year. I dug in my sophomore year to learn; I bought the guidebooks and better maps, read blogs, and joined Facebook groups. I became an expert my junior year by adding more overnight hikes and upgrading gear. As a senior, I realized I had a hiking tree (like an NFL coaching tree) as six of my hiking partners were now very serious about the 48. Three have finished and will also be at the banquet. Another will finish in 2016, the other two in 2017.

During my quest to complete the 48 I also found myself identifying "Bucket List" hiking adventures. I just returned from Wyoming where I took on the Grand Tetons and Yellowstone National Park. I hiked 40+ miles over three days seeing some of the country's best landscapes. I also hit Yosemite and, a month ago, completed a full Presidential Traverse with a night at the Lakes of the Clouds Hut (my first hut stay). And while these adventures and the 48 have been personally satisfying and rewarding, they have also played a very healthy role in my family life.

My wife and kids are proud of me. I know it; I could see it and feel it in their unflinching support of the 48. I know hiking has made me a better father, a better husband. While on trail I think how fortunate I am to have the family I have and it's been very easy for me to give back to them. To thank them for allowing me to follow and achieve this. I also believe, on some level, I've inspired them to set goals and dream big for themselves. Plus, my relationships with my hiking partners have evolved to a point that they can be considered family. Put it on the board. Viva the 48.

NAME: KEITH GENTILI                                              AGE: 48

TOWN/STATE: NEW BOSTON, NH 03070          AMC MEMBER: YES

# GRADUATION: THE NEXT PEAK

My application for the Appalachian Mountain Club Four Thousand Footer Club graduation ceremony celebrating its Class of 2015 was accepted. I was indeed going to the dance. I couldn't help but start making plans surrounding the event, which was scheduled for April 16, 2016 at Exeter, NH, High School.

First, I needed to confirm my hiking partners would also be at the dance. Reimer and Unger, both tremendously efficient in their day-to-day lives, finished their NH 48 together on October 1 and had taken care of business. Their applications were well in by the New Year and they both had their tickets punched. Yes, the New Boston Dads would be dancing.

Hanson finished his NH 48 on Mount Isolation on September 20, a week before me, and certainly in time to secure his spot in the Class of 2015. However, my concern was he wouldn't get his application done, that it would fall off his radar and he would miss the deadline. Hanson and I climbed 30 of the NH 48 mountains together and our hiking history went back 25 years to Fitchburg State. I'm not sure I would have completed the NH 48 without Hanson. His presence at graduation was non-negotiable to me, and I encouraged him to get his essay written. I even emailed him my essay for inspiration, motivation, and as a reminder to get it done. In the end, he got it done. Hanson, too, would be dancing.

"For me, it was always 'I'll do the New Hampshire 48 someday,'" said Hanson. "But when you actually complete it, and look back on it, it's a big commitment. There's no 'I'll do one here and one there.' You'll never get it done that way."

Engler had his own challenges. With just three peaks to go, he tweaked his knee on a failed solo hike of Isolation in December. He got caught in some deep snow and felt something. It's not uncommon for hikers to suffer stingers in their knees but this set him back a month. Engler was forced to rest his knee and wasn't able to finish his NH 48 in 2015. He did, however, stay committed to completing his journey.

On January 31, 2016, Engler summited Isolation alone in a snowstorm. I was hiking Killington (VT) that day with Reimer and Unger in pursuit of our New England 67 and was texting him all day.

I was really worried about him being out solo in those conditions. The following day, February 1, 2016, he climbed Waumbek. When he reached the parking lot, he drove straight to Waterville Valley, and hiked up and down Tecumseh. Engler was done. He was a 48er. But would he dance with his buddies? He was the one guy who always hiked to be with his friends, not necessarily for the time on trail.

"In my application, I told the AMC that my focus was not on hiking the peaks. It was on being with my buddies, and all of my buddies are going to the dance in April and I'm worried I'm not going to the dance," said Engler. "But I told them when I finished my hikes and hoped to make their cutoff time. When I was accepted, I was ecstatic."

I was, and remain, immensely proud of Engler for completing his NH 48 journey. It didn't come easy to him. He is an individual in the truest sense of the word. The fact he came along for this ride with me (and the others) speaks volumes about his character and will always connect us. We climbed 25 of these 48 mountains together and shared all of the highs and lows that come with the territory. I am grateful for his company and honored to have been at his side through the journey.

"I am super proud of finishing the 48," said Engler. "It was not originally a goal of mine. I am not someone who has goals or is goal-oriented."

As April 16 neared, and with all five of us confirmed for the dance, I was able to begin planning the evening. I booked a few outdoor tables at Throwback Brewery in North Hampton, NH. Just a 15-minute ride from Exeter High School, Throwback would be the ideal spot to pregame and meet for a few beers and appetizers. I also wanted to show each of the guys how much I appreciated their role in my road to 48. This would be the opportunity to do that. I printed my favorite group photo of each of them, framed it, and dropped it into a gift bag to be presented at Throwback.

On Saturday, April 16, 2016, Reimer, Unger, and I all loaded up our families in the afternoon and made the drive from New Boston to North Hampton. I wore my 48 Peaks shirt. Engler and his wife Kelli joined us there. Hanson arrived solo as Hannah was home with their two young children. We sat outdoors and our kids had a ball enjoying the farm setting. Between the field, the chickens, and the snacks, they were thoroughly entertained.

Meanwhile the adults were enjoying Throwback's Donkey-Hoté Double IPA and recounting our tales from the mountains. Not surprisingly, I got emotional when handing out the framed photos and congratulating them on their NH 48.

"Throwback was awesome. It was a beautiful night," said Hanson. "Being outside on the back patio enjoying some beers. I still have my photo in my office."

"I was really happy for you," Engler told me. "I have that photo on my desk. Thank you. It really was a hiking club moment, a graduation moment."

Engler, being both introspective and a button pusher, added the following thoughts on the five of us and the evolution of our NH 48.

"It really opened up a whole new world for me. One I never imagined. I never would of thought of hiking the 48," he said. "Your persistence with it. Your perseverance. Between the Fitchburg State Hiking Club as well as Ron and Jake, and your other New Boston friends, we had a real hiking network. We'd be like, 'He just did that mountain, we gotta keep up.' It was awesome.

"Of course, Hanson and I would 'dis' you for hiking with the New Boston guys. We'd call them the kids as they were younger than us and they hiked fast. We'd laugh. I couldn't keep up with the kids."

It was here I apologized to Engler for cheating on him and Hanson. But I told him it was their fault. Hanson was always late and he hiked too slow. Meanwhile, Unger's making movies about us and Reimer's crushing peaks from Lake Placid to Katahdin. Ha. This was one of our final exchanges in the making of *White Mountains State* and it might just be my favorite moment from the entire interview process.

The New Boston families departed Throwback for Exeter High School to participate in the banquet portion of the evening, which included pizza and salad in the cafeteria. The Englers and Hanson would catch up with us later. While standing in line to enter the event and chatting with Unger, a gentleman approached us and said, "I like your T-shirt." He was talking to Unger, who was wearing a Russian River Brewing T-shirt featuring its award-winning IPA, Pliny the Elder. Seems my 48 Peaks shirt went unnoticed.

That night, nearly 900 hikers were recognized across the AMC's six lists including the New Hampshire 48. The Exeter High School auditorium was standing room only and it was a special night. The presentation was tastefully done and the folks in attendance knew it.

"At first, I was thinking it would be like a Boy Scout awards ceremony. No big deal," said Hanson. "But the way they do it, it's really nice. Seeing our photos during the slide show was so cool."

I had submitted both a Fitchburg State Hiking Club and a New Boston Dads summit photo. Both made the cut and were part of the event's slideshow. It was a surprise and our group let out some raucous applause when they appeared on screen. It made me happy, and the moment reminded me that my NH 48 was more about people than mountains. It didn't start that way, but it certainly ended that way. It was unmistakable.

"The most important thing is the people you are hiking with," Engler once said. "And the people you are thinking about when you are hiking."

It took me four years to complete the *White Mountains State* curriculum and graduate. I was 48 years old when an AMC staffer handed me my diploma. It took me eight years to get through Fitchburg State. Both institutions delivered people into my life that will be with me forever.

Ron Reimer, Jason Unger, me, Eric Hanson, and Eric Engler at graduation

# RESOURCES

The following are the most common resources used by the author in planning and preparing for each of the hikes detailed in the book. Please note all hikes were planned between 2012 and 2015.

## MAPS

1. Exploring New Hampshire's White Mountains Waterproof TOPO Map & Guide, The Wilderness Map Company

2. White Mountains Waterproof Trail Map (5th Edition), Map Adventures

## BOOKS

1. *Hiker's Guide to the Mountains of New Hampshire* by Jared Gange

2. *The 4000-Footers of the White Mountains* by Steven D. Smith & Mike Dickerman

3. *Appalachian Mountain Club White Mountain Guide (29th Edition\*)* by Steven D. Smith & Mike Dickerman

\*In October 2022, the AMC published its 31st Edition of its *White Mountain Guide*.

## WEBSITES – TRAILS, TRAIL REPORTS

1. 4000footers.com

2. newenglandtrailconditions.com/nh

3. trailsnh.com/dashboard.php

4. facebook.com/groups/hikenh4k

## WEBSITES – WEATHER

1. mountain-forecast.com

2. mountwashington.org/experience-the-weather/higher-summit-forecast. aspx

# ACKNOWLEDGMENTS

The author thanks his hiking partners—Eric Hanson, Eric Engler, Keith Rice, Jason Unger, Ron Reimer, Jamie Neefe, Tom Fraser, and Kevin Bell—for sharing their New Hampshire 48 memories and thoughts with readers. He realizes he was a bit of a bully at times in hunting each of them down on multiple occasions and forcing them to answer his questions about hikes that took place seven to 10 years ago.

The author also thanks his family—Carrie, Julia, and Sarah—for their unwavering support and encouragement of this project. In particular, he wishes to recognize his daughter Sarah for being his rubber duck during the process and for ending many conversations with a "Shouldn't you be writing your book?"

Finally, the author would like to thank the following individuals for their interest in and contribution to *White Mountains State*: Daniel Guarino, Stephen Herdman, Eric Jackel, Peter Johnson, David Litwinovich, Ed Murray, and Ted Walsh.

# ABOUT THE AUTHOR

Keith Gentili is a lifelong hiker, writer, and editor. In addition to climbing New Hampshire's 48 tallest mountains, he has summited New England's 100 highest peaks. Gentili has also completed four of New Hampshire's signature hikes including the Wapack Trail, Presidential Traverse, Pemi Loop, and Monadnock-Sunapee Greenway. He is halfway through his Winter NH 48, climbed Maine's Katahdin four times, and is slowly working on redlining Acadia National Park.

A former sportswriter, Gentili launched *The New Boston Beacon*, a monthly newspaper, in 2018. The New Hampshire Press Association has named him a Columnist of the Year three times. In 2021, the New England Press Association honored *The Beacon* as a Distinguished Newspaper and Gentili as a Serious Columnist of the Year. His publishing background also includes years with the *Nantucket Beacon*, *Tuff Stuff* magazine, and Antiques Roadshow *Insider*.

In his free time, Gentili still enjoys playing with baseball cards and in 2022, he began working for Topps Trading Cards. A graduate of Fitchburg State College, Gentili lives in New Boston, NH, with his wife Carrie and their daughters Julia and Sarah.

CPSIA information can be obtained
at www.ICGtesting.com
Printed in the USA
JSHW051916281022
32219JS00005B/17